BETWEEN THE RIVER AND THE STARS

By

TONY MAUDE

*Had I not become a man,
I might as well have been a swan,
Living happy ever after,
Between the river and the stars.*

FIRST EDITION

Little Red Tree Publishing, LLC,
635 Ocean Avenue, New London, CT 06320

Copyright © 2013 Tony Maude

All rights are reserved under International and Pan-American Copyright Conventions. Except for brief passages quoted in a newspaper, magazine, radio or television review, no part of this book may be reproduced in any form or by any means, electronic or mechanical, including photocopying and recording, or by any information storage and retrieval system, without permission in writing from the author or publisher.

Layout and Cover Design: Michael John Linnard, MCSD
Text in New Time Roman, Trajan Pro and Ariel.

First Edition, 2013, manufactured in USA
1 2 3 4 5 6 7 8 9 10 LSI 20 19 18 17 16 15 14 13

Photograph of Tony Maude on page 150 and the back cover appears by kind permission of Ray Conway.

All illustrations and photographs, not otherwise attributed, printed in this book are by the kind permission of Tony Maude.

"All White Cat" (page 17) - Winner of Bill Winter Award, 2002 - Poetry on the Lake, Orta, Italy (www.poetryonthelake.com)

Library of Congress Cataloging-in-Publication Data:

Maude, Tony
  Between the River and the Stars / by Tony Maude. -- 1st ed.
     p. cm.
  Includes glossary.
  Includes index.
  ISBN-13: 978-1-935656-25-8 (pbk. : alk. paper)
  I. Title.
  PS3619.O4326C55 2011
  811'.6--dc22

Little Red Tree Publishing, LLC
635 Ocean Avenue,
New London, CT 06320
website: www.littleredtree.com

Acknowledgements

There are a number of people who have been part of this book.

John Shirbon and Michael Linnard who set the project in motion.

Betty Worthington, who lived alone in the Owl House and was the first person to hear the poem "Without Surprise."

Joan Kent, Diana Miller, Marianne Mikkelsen and Teresa who kept every poem I sent them.

Seamus Hosey, (RTE Radio, Ireland), Colum Sands, (BBC Radio Ulster), Guido Leotta, Mauro Quai and Lino Straulino (Italian branch)! Peter Bennett and Heide Rohloff, (Germany), Sean Sexton, Fionnuala Tuohy, Marie O'Neill and Don, (Ennis and Belfast).

To my publisher, Michael Linnard of Little Red Tree Publishing, New London, Connecticut, USA, for over-riding my reservations about allowing these poems to "Leave the stage!" and appear in the far harsher spot-light of "The Page."

And finally, to Marjorie and Bruce Maude…

> "Since I can remember, I could not make up my mind,
>   Walking to school took me all day.
> There was something in the hedgerow I might have left behind,
>   And that yearning never stopped or went away..."

CONTENTS

Introduction by Tony Maude   ix

Chapter 1 — America

July 4, 2013	2
Trilogy About America	3
Cave Carvings	6

Chapter 2 – Kids, Cats and God's Creatures

Change of Plea	10
Answers on a Postcard	12
River of Kids	13
Alan & Luke	14
Callum's Story	15
Butterflies / Soldiers	16
All White Cat	17
Arcadia	18
Double Take	19
House Martins	20
Must Go Home	21
Charlie Blue	22
Concentrate!	24
Great Spotted or Green and Decker	24
Catdream	25
A River with G	26
No Webs!	27
Without Surprise	28
Midnight Feast	30

Chapter 3 — The Isle of Emerald, Ruby and Rainbows

In a Saucepan	32
Faery Tale, Connemara	33
...Street Deal	36
Monarch of the Roof-tops	37

Ennis Summer	38
Fifteen Miles	39
Yeats' Tower	40
Kilsheelan Bridge	41
Wrote a Carol for the Radio	42
Serious Rain	43
Recording the Sea	44
To Ireland	45
The Isle of Emerald, Ruby and...	48
All Night Story	49
On Tour in Ulster	50
Comedy of Manners	52

Chapter 4 – Merrie England – Green and Pleasant Land

Another River Song	54
Autumn	55
Standing Stone – Cornwall – Fourth Century A.D.	56
Ely Cathedral	57
The Five Sisters Window	59
There Was a Time Before the TV	60
Hackpen Hill-Avebury	61
The Rollright Stones	62
Spelsbury Church	63
For the Spelsbury Children	65
Gig at Froyle Mill	66
The Peddars Way	67

Merrie England – London Branch

Christmas Cheer in Dryburgh Road, Putney	70
Whirligig	71
Dalmatian	72
London Thunder	73
"ROLL of HONOUR" For Two World Wars	74
New Neighbours	75
No Time	75
Run of the Mill	76

Chapter 5 — The Road, The Show and "The Music"

If All the Music...	78
A Gig	79
The Poetry Festival	80
The Music	82
Medieval Music — Hanover Station	83
German Fairy-Tale Winter Tour	84

Chapter 6 — The Whole Business... of Poetry

Presentation	88
Poets	89
Treasurer	90
Pencil	91
To Draw Or Not To Draw	92
Lines from the Underground	93
Et Tu Leonardo?	94
Paths to the Sun	95

Chapter 7 — Comedy Spot

Make a List, Lest Ye Be Lost	98
Bedside Companions	98
Jealousy	99
DON BE 100	100
Only Joking	101
New Life Resolution	101
JAK 359W	102
Occupation:	104
Jumpers	106

Chapter 8 — "This Dark World and Wide"

Short Fruity Poem	108
The Rose Thief	109
Icon	110
Names of Trees	111

Anything That's Going!	112
Seven Years to Draw a Swan	114
From the Track Through the Pines to the Copper Sea	119
Radio	123
Poem For Mr. Boyd - the Poet	124
Answering Dad Back	126
Glossary	128
Index of Titles and First Lines	144
About the Poet	150

INTRODUCTION

*"Man is least himself when he talks in his own person.
Give him a mask, and he will tell you the truth."*
Oscar Wilde

Having said that, here are a few facts, a bit of background, a word or two in my ...own person, to introduce this book. I owe that to Little Red Tree Publishing for kindly persuading me, after many years of pencil-sharpening and chewing, to finally put these poems on a page. Such a poem is only "half a poem" according to Dylan Thomas and, in tune with this notion, I have spent the aforesaid many years, learning by heart and performing those ones that it seemed would feel at home in "A Show."

I was born in India, a hill-station seven thousand feet above the sea and beside a boat-skimmed lake with, in the background, blue and strange-shaped mountains. Not a bad place to greet the World. My Dad was an Army-Man, and the nomadic life we led put me ashore at boarding-schools in green and pleasant parts of England... and, at the first of these, when I was eleven, my career as storyteller and poet began.

After "Lights Out" in a dormitory of ten or so beds, with a very fine view over Surrey and Sussex to the South Downs and their promise of the coast beyond, I would tell stories to my fellows. A serial that went on night after night — I can't imagine how I managed thus to spin it out! "My Life in India" was the title, and seeing that the family had left for England shortly before I was two, my memories must have been scanty, if indeed I had any. The truth is that these stories were all based on those my grand-mother told me: picking fruit before breakfast and coming face to face in the mango tree with an awakening and uncoiling cobra... or... the time when a circling eagle crashed down and went off with one of the kittens. All this was just before I came across Shakespeare, on an outing from the same school: Julius Caesar at Guildford Theatre. The play held my interest well until, towards the end, Mark Antony tells us: "This was the noblest Roman of them all..." a speech which ends with "...that nature might stand up and say to all the world, this was a man!" These words acted as introduction, became companions, said "Come along," thus handing me a key to the secret garden.

Just before I went to university, I found myself in Paris on the way back from hitching down to Spain. A concert at Olympia — the great theatre of "La Chanson Poétique," whose songs I loved then and still do: Georges Brassens, Jacques Brel, Anne Sylvestre… Barbara. That night, however, they had guests from abroad: The Everly Brothers, supported by Peter, Paul and Mary. I'd heard the latter's sweet and harmonious versions of folk songs but that night they introduced a song by a "new, young songwriter from the USA"—during which, came the words: "ain't no use in turnin' on your light Babe, the light I never knowed… ain't no use in… I'm on the dark side of the road…"—this was another "noblest Roman" moment. That "…dark side of the road" was to me, a revelation. In this way, Paris (France!) '63, I was introduced to Bob Dylan.

Dylan Thomas, I already knew: "A Child's Christmas in Wales" for one thing, which my Mum and I watched on TV and were taken utterly in thrall. These landmark experiences kept coming and must have made me decide: "I'd better start writing things down myself." It all began for Thomas, he said, with Nursery Rhymes – how, before he understood their meaning, the very *sounds* of the words captivated him. I'd agree, but after sounds came **Stories** and with them an added sense of Poetry:

> My old Auntie Stella,
> May God and all the Angels bless her,
> Was the first person to say to me
> The word, what she called "Poi-etry:"
> "The Knights of the Four Winds,"
> Gonsalves was the man:
> Serpents, Damsels, Oceans, Snows…
> And then she went on to read me:
> "*Wild Animals I Have Known**" and
> "*The Trail of The Sandhill Stag**," that's
> Poetry! Handfuls of words like-dice-thrown,
> That look you in the eye and say "Listen… listen!"

*books by Ernest Thompson Seton, American conservationist.

I went to Oxford University in '63 to pursue my love of language and literature "officially." It was also then that I began writing songs for Cabaret Shows, with many a later-to-become-famous artiste, including some of the Monty Python team. Every time I go back, I'm amazed by the beauty of the place, and equally troubled by the feeling: what a shame I couldn't appreciate it while I was there. Just the other day, looking up at my "rooms" at New College (Kris Kristofferson also went there), I noticed a small and exquisite stone carving beneath the Gothic arch of my window: a medieval piper, with cloak and hood who must have always been there. I couldn't believe that I'd missed him during all those years! Although I suppose,

> In the rough and tumble of those days,
> I may well not have seen him but
> On some Summer's or Winter's night,
> How can I not have heard him play?

Once released from the academic life, I moved to London and began playing, singing and writing songs. I was involved with running a show from 1968 to 1976, at the world-famous Troubadour Club, Earl's Court, with Nigel Barker, poet and songwriter. "Everyone" has played there: Bob Dylan, Paul Simon... you name! Tom Paxton came down one night and regaled us. It was there I met and became friends with many of the musicians with whom I was to work and record thereafter: Paul Millns, who produced my first two albums and plays inspired keyboards on all three for "Autogram," Germany. Shusha, who recorded my settings of Elizabethan poets on various successful records, Tony Bird who amazed us all: his guitar style, his voice and songs overflowing with the beauty, the sadness, the sounds and the colours of Africa, and not least, the publisher of this book, who was then part of the brilliant guitar duo "Linnard and Hughes."

During this time, I wrote the occasional poem – have a look at "Christmas Cheer in Dryburgh Road, Putney." (page 70) This follows a strict rhyme scheme (unusual for me!) and is dedicated to John Betjeman. My poems were then few and far between, being too busy as a singer-songwriter. Year after year, I toured on the continent—Germany and Holland at first and later in Italy—always at the wheel of an old Ford van: "You mean you drove this here, all the way from London?!" "I did... and I'll be driving it back there again!!"

I'm no good at dates but I know *this* one, it was in 1988 that I "seriously" began writing and performing poems. The poem that started this new lease begins: "Written for Ben on his Birthday." With this poem

"Without Surprise" (page 28) and one or two others, I tried my luck in the London Poetry Clubs, and was amazed that I was offered a booking in the first one I went to. Subsequently, I performed throughout London and beyond as the "main guest" and for this I was occasionally paid!

It's actually no surprise that the breakthrough poem (above) is steadfastly based in the Natural World, as are many others in this collection – it was Auntie Stella, again, who taught me:

> In the voices of the forest
> Firmly to believe
>
> And that "Poi-etry" is to be enjoyed!

There was a school anthology we used called "Poems for Pleasure." I'm sorry but what else would they be for? As Feste, the clown sings in Twelfth Night: "We'll strive to please you everyday…" And this has been a trusty guide in my attitude to "The Business of Poetry." In this sense, a poem is like a joke – you can't enjoy it if you don't get it.

Some enlightened person had left money to pay a different writer every year to come to my second boarding school and read us their work. One of these was John Betjeman and *his* evening far out-stripped the others. It was a Performance, a Tour-de-Force which began with a magnificent "ice-breaker" – for the whole story, I'm afraid you'll have to wait for Volume 2, as the poem thereon is still in the making. That evening was another landmark, another "I see!" Another "So, that's the way!!"

I often think of poems in terms of what I call "Village Hall." I imagine—I or we—have been booked to entertain all and sundry this very evening. The place will be packed – people from all walks and of all ages. The show will go fine if we speak from the heart, with music and drama, some tears/some humour, take them on a journey, make it clear, push the boundaries so they go home happy and come back next week/month/year… for more.

~~~~

A wonderful poem by George Herbert begins

> "When God at first made man,
> Having a glass of blessings standing by…"

I once won a "recite by heart" competition with this as set text. I can still remember most of it, especially the phrase "glass of blessings" i.e. man's qualities crammed into a glass, ready for God to bestow as he wished. This made me think of the "Glass of The Arts" and Poetry's position in it. Recently, I heard a radio programme on Dance and the spokeswoman described her calling as the "Cinderella" of the Arts — in terms of funding, interest, and support. In a way, she may be right, when you think of the cash poured into opera, classical music and theatre, not to mention "The World of Fine Art Painting!" However, if Dance is the Cinderella, what's Poetry then? The Ugly Sister? The mouse in the corner…?? Try to imagine the Sydney Opera House changed to Sydney Poetry House! However, I suggest that there are many more people with a small part of their souls reserved for perhaps just one poem, or maybe just a line… than are those familiar with even the most famous Puccini aria… Here is an example:

> "At the going down of the sun and in the morning,
> We shall remember them."

Taken from "For the Fallen" by Robert Laurence Binyon

This line was suggested by an elderly member of a Poetry/Music workshop in Ireland and acted as a key for other members of the group to remember close-to-their-heart lines and poems.

Here I should add, with some respect towards those who run the show, that I have found poetry to be largely the domain...

> Of Old People and Children,
> For instance, the poem "NO WEBS" (page 27)
> Was first published in the garden.
> I wrote the so-called Proclamation on
> A sawn-off piece of skirting-board and
> Hung it on the apple tree. Many "Humans"
> Passed that way, all well-established adults—
> The poem was neither read nor noticed by a soul,
> Till: enter, wide-eyed, Freddie from Cornwall.

> He was ten or eleven and the first to mention it,
> That goes for the spiders an' all, for whom
> It was written, not one of them
> Paid a blind bit of notice! With this piece
> Of evidence I... rest my case.

As regards the title of this book, "...The Stars" speak for themselves but from an early age I have been vociferously speaking for and about "The River..." When I was seven, a refined and kindly old gentleman — Major Stanley-Clark, used to take me for walks along the River Wey: summer evenings, setting sun, herons, swans, bits of fishing-line or "is it a spider's web?" that must have been when it all began. Here are a few highlighted references to rivers from the poems in this book:

> "the black-ink glinting water" (the Rhine in Winter, page 84)
> "wandering weeds and bubbling beads philosophy... polish your stones and whistle your tunes... and take it easy."
> (the river Wey in all seasons, page 54)

Some years ago, I visited Stratford—the home of William Shakespeare—paddling downstream from Warwick along the river Avon. One night I went to the famous theatre by canoe, from the camping site, half a mile upstream. The play I saw was a walkabout through the town and surrounding fields, in which the audience was encouraged to buy huge "medieval" tar torches to help light the procession's way. At the end, people discarded them in a scattered, giant-matchstick bonfire. I took one, still burning, tied it to a cross-member in the canoe and paddled "home" along the Avon.

> Sending shadows and shards of gold
> Skimming over the dark water,
> Into the overhanging foliage
> And up to the summer's night stars

And finally:

A fine river runs across County Clare—the Fergus—it winds its way through many a lake and out to the Atlantic at Clarecastle. I was once swimming alone by an old stone bridge and was spied by a swan, which had cruised up through one of the arches. With seven cygnets downstream, he or she was furious to see this intruder and came towards me, wings beating and spitting fire.

Having just emerged from the water, dripping and naked, I stood my ground and said: "Ok, Ok, I understand, but these waters are to share, this is also *my* river."

> Had I not become a man,
> I might as well have been a swan,
> Living happy ever after.
> Between the River and the Stars.

You will no doubt notice that I have used a good number of quotes from others in this introduction. This I consider to be essential to show what inspired, what pushed the boat out and trumpeted the sense of "not alone."

Here, to finish, is a quick true-story, which in part sums up my "life as a poet." Forgive me, but to fully understand this you'll have to refer to the last poem in the book ahead: "Answering Dad Back" (Page 126).

At one of my shows in a Belfast Psychiatric Hospital, which included this poem, a young man approached me at the end of the gig. He had a faraway expression, which, before he spoke, came suddenly into focus. He looked me in the eye and with somewhere between a smile and a frown, said simply: "…and managed to write it down."

> "So what *have* I achieved?
> No feat of great renown but
> I've seen the visible world
> on a winter's dawn
> And managed…
> to write it down."

Tony Maude
London, England 2013

*For Lucy H, Kate and Teresa L,
But as everyone knows, it's
bad form to point out Angels.*

CHAPTER 1

AMERICA

Some song lyrics **inspired by America**
As "a thank-you" to my American publisher.

July 4, 2013

Now that Russell Hoban's gone,
It's up to us to carry on.
Now Kerouac's not coming back,
Let's drive life like a Cadillac.
"Why all these Americans?"
"Right! Here's a verse for Betjeman:
Now Sir John resides on high,
It's up to us to versify.
Now Jacques Brel has moved along,
We must belt out heart-felt songs.
Now there's no more Lenny Bruce,
We must try and let truth loose.
To end this verse where it began:
The wondrous work of Russell Hoban,
Live the spirit of Riddley Walker,
In tune, alongside Mother Nature,
Curious, brave, walk through the rain,
Go your own, be wise and shine.

With thanks to William Blake:

"A robin red-breast in a cage
Puts all Heaven in a rage."

Written on July 4, 2013, as I drove away from London, along the M3 Motorway. Let's then make it a Poem for America - partly in view of the auspicious date and partly as I was headin' that way... OK! Not exactly Route 66... but south-west and out of town... get there before sun-down?

TRILOGY ABOUT AMERICA

1] The Landscape of America.

The landscape of America
Is mapped out in songs
Mapped out in highways and trains:
That Ol' 66, the Rock Island Line…
The City of New Orleans
And the spirit of the "Indian,"
That's what we used to call
The people of the canyons and forests,
The deserts and waterfalls.

2] The Music of America

They get a lot of stick and a lot of it's deserved,
It's a hard to handle land,
From snowy old Alaska, past the prairies and the plains
To California's golden sands.

They came from Scotland and Ireland
With their jigs and their reels,
They came from Scandinavia with their fiddles and their bows,
They came with Balalaikas and boxes you can squeeze
And from Africa with their rhythms and their soul.

And that's America… you got a lot to answer for,
'Twas on the banks of the Seine,
He picked up his guitar and with a laaazy smile,
He said "Weiall… here we go again!"

He sang about the rail-roads, he sang about the rain,
He sang about the places where them chilly winds don't blow.
He sang about New Orleans and he sang about the mines
And he sang about the buffalo.

And a woman stood beside him, she had burnt-sienna skin
…she played an old banjo
An' every step of every song she kept in tune and right in time
And sang every word he sang one third below.

And that's America…a lot to answer for,
'Twas by the towers of Notre Dame,
I could have been a rich man — two cars and a lawn,
If I'd never heard that music play.

When I was just a little kid, with my wind-up gramophone,
Frank Marvin kept me company when I was all alone—
"I don't Work for a Living," that song took me in thrall,
Frank Marvin's got a lot to answer for an' all!

An' all these guys called Hank: Williams, Thompson, Snow
With voices like train whistles and their eyes tight closed,
They made me buy my first guitar, a Harmony Monterey,
Just like the one Muddy Waters used to play.

Hey! America, the first songs I learned to play—
The Midnight Special… Jesse James…
The name of my guitars and the game was "Harmony"
Though: "In some lonesome valley, poor boy you're bound to die."

3]   The Finger-Pickers of America

Here's to the Finger-Pickers of America,
They found this thing as fine as A B C—
Took tunes from Ireland, Africa… all over
An' boiled 'em in a pot called Tennessee.

It's so darn cool… so damn fine and easy,
Your thumb plays bass… can everybody see?
And when it's rollin' reg'lar as a freight train,
Your fingers put in… the filigree

So here's to the Finger-Pickers of America,
One day they must have found some old guitar
And put on strings of steel like three rail-roads,
They knew that train would shine and travel far

It travelled south along the Alabama plains,
The Bluesmen said "We can use that… thank'ye kindly!"
On through Cajun Country down to New Orleans
And out along them old Florida Keys.

A calypso man in Key West singing "Yellow Bird,"
Finger-picked to while away the hours,
To F-F-F Fabe… that's what I call poetry,
It's what Dylan meant by "…fishermen hold flowers."

Here's to all Finger-pickers, to all Troubadours,
Les Comédiens, les Musiciens, God bless 'em all
As through the rain they travel, in trains and rusty cars,
Set up their tunes on windy market stalls.

In 1934 Huddie William "Lead Belly" Ledbetter recorded a version of the song, "The Midnight Special," at Angola Prison for John and Alan Lomax, who mistakenly attributed it to him as the author. Publicity photo in the Public domain.

To conclude this chapter on America, the final paragraph from *Cave Carvings in the Capitol* (1996). This is a sketched account of a short tour in the Mid-West—my first and only visit to the USA—one man's week performing two people's poems, playing music and learning about America.

During this time, I came across a museum in Madison and was captivated by an Ojibway painting in the foyer. What I thought would be a *quick look round*, became at least a couple of hours making notes and sketches. This was my introduction to the Spirit and Things of the *Lake & Forest* Native Americans.

CAVE CARVINGS

And in our World where concrete, steel, glass and neon
Have more or less anesthetized the seasons,
The Ojibway speak of the weeks of the Crisp Crust Snow
and the month of the Ricing Moon.

The wild rice that grows by the lake
and falls into working boats when shaken.
I was given a hint of Lakota Sioux (of the Dakota's)

"Me—tdock—ou—yay—oh—yay—see"
Means: "You are all my relations — we are all one family"

Please… make yourself known, anyone
Who doesn't agree.

Pictorial notation of an Ojibway music board. Original illustration on birchwood slab, collected in northern Great Lakes area, c1820, drawn by Capt. S. Eastman, U.S. Army.

Portrait of a great Ojibway medicine man, Shawwanossoway, by Paul Kane, 1845, oil on paper.

Ojibway women harvest a crop in late September. The woman in the stern paddled while the others collected the rice, c1857, watercolor version by Capt. S. Eastman, U.S. Army.

CHAPTER 2

KIDS, CATS AND GOD'S CREATURES

CHANGE OF PLEA

Your 'onour I admit, I am to blame!
I did lead the children astray when they
Should be thinking of tests and lists
Of jobs and universities, I
Gathered them up and went via the woods
Down to the sparkling sea…
Suggested that they swim their fill,
Search for flowers in the rocks,
Find trails made by the fins of fish
And follow the footprints of otters—
Watch for foxes in the distant hills,
Trace patterns in the waves and frost,
Observe the appearance of the stars
And listen out for owls…

Led them up the garden path
Away from the Curriculum and thus
Wholeheartedly sanctioned the notion
Of turning a blind eye to exams – I am
Also guilty of encouraging them
To see figures in the fire and hawthorn,
To sing and learn by heart: "Brandy for the parson,
Baccy for the clerk…"* Introduced them on the quay
To the (what shall we do?) Drunken Sailor,
Thus setting wayward thoughts in motion

Make him:

"Dance with a shark in the deepest ocean,
Ride a butterfly up to Heaven,
Sail a sieve across the Moon,
Earlie in the morning.

Brush his teeth with a vacuum cleaner,
Wash his hair with an April shower,
Shine his shoes with a four–leaf clover,
Earlie in the morning."

None of us has a leg to stand on,
Making sails and assembling wings,
Like Icarus with
one eye on the ocean
but the other working out
our distance from the Sun.

A line from Rudyard Kipling's "A Smugglers Song."

ANSWERS ON A POSTCARD

Who was the first to look at the sky
And wonder how the Moon hovers and wanders,
Or does it dangle from invisible wires?
And while we're on this,
Who was the one,
Who first
Put a match to the sun?

And talking of wires, who was the person
Who designed the spider? Taught it how
To cast a rope across the garden,
Gauge the wind and aim so fine
And fix it like a washing line
Of silk (as bright), of steel (as strong)
To hang its dangerous, most ingenious,
Geometric house on?

And while still on this... ... anyone?
Who first
Put a match to the Sun?

RIVER OF KIDS

For the children (red uniforms) and the staff of Clarecastle School, West of Ireland. Three classes were crammed into one for my Concert in the Afternoon. Over a hundred children where there would normally be thirty....

There were spider kids poised in the corners
Leopard ones lounging in trees,
Congregation children sitting in rows,
Batkids in the eaves.
Cockroach children crouched on the floor,
Some "nice as ninepence" in buttons and bows,
And Will I or Won't I's? Outside the door,
Circus children standing on shoulders.
The room was loaded to the rafters,
To the gunwales (the very edge of the boat)
And all in red, like devils or foxes,
Cardinals, robins or stoats.
Cardboard kids cut out for greatness?
Or run-of-the-mill? "You never know!"
But I tell you, I was glad to see them,
Rolling up and in to see the show.

ALAN & LUKE

An old, shaggy, black and white dog
Who, when encouraged, can just jump up
To well above your knees, lean
On you with spiky claws
And look you in the eyes.

"That's my dog!" said Alan (who's four).
"Is he?" I replied, "He's a fine one and
 He's a good jumper!"

"That's not a jumper!" said Alan,
"That's not a jumper, that's his skin!"

As we listened, wide-eyed, the way
You watch a flash of lightning.

CALLUM'S STORY

The boy who likes eggs for their own sake
And who loves colour as well.
So, at Easter he wanted one for its shape
And it had to be purple.

He showed it to another lad
Aged about six an'all,
Who had a host of presents for Easter,
A veritable armful:
Guns and trucks…. remote controls, so

When he saw the egg, scratched his head
and trying to think it through,
said: "Does it calculate…does it climb boulders?
What does it *do*?!"

And Callum unperturbed, no fuss,
Absolutely cool,
Said: "Es sieht schoen aus,"
(translated): "It…….looks beautiful."

BUTTERFLIES / SOLDIERS

      Butterflies fly in a wobbly way

                As though they don't know
    where they're
going, they
        lurch and slide all   over
                            the
                  place, as though
      They're flying on oil or   ICE!   But
    In their upandown   roundabout
way, they're

        Guided by
  immense grace. Thank God
         they
           Don't have to go on parade: Stand up,
Shut up!

                And hold a rifle…

    with great respect
  To Butterflies, a Butterfly Squad would
      Be *A SHAMBLES!!*

But **Crows** would make fantastic soldiers,
Looking neither to left nor right,
In their single-minded, world-famous,
Unwavering flight… … … … …
Building Roman roads across the Heavens.
They also have at their disposal
A deadly built-in weapon… … … … …

And **Ants** are soldiers anyway,
With their muscly, bossy, "Get out my way!"
Their uniform, their "Watch it mate!"
Ferocious bite and armour-plate.
I think that we can safely say,
An ant is at the other end of the rainbow
From a butterfly.

ALL WHITE CAT

I came across, in my lined diary,
A blank page.
How had it managed to slip through the net?
To outwit the printer? Side-step the relentless rollers?
It was a silent glade in a busy wood,
But I described it as an all white cat,
Who finds itself, by surprise,
Wandering towards the horizon,
Among endless, rulered rows of vines.

ARCADIA

                Though
I say it myself, I have
a beautiful garden.

"Were you responsible? Did you
make it that way?"

                "Well, no,
I only stumbled upon it, tapped
and nudged it
in that direction."

DOUBLE TAKE

I went into the garden late
And thought it was an owl;
In fact, it was a long, pale cat,
Bolt upright on the wall.

"Hello!" I said, "What brings you here
This soft, damp summer's night?"

And the cat moved never a whisker,
To acknowledge even that I was there –
Come to think, to such a trivial question,
What cat would deign to answer?

Had I asked something *interesting*,
Like "What kind of purse would fit the Moon?
Could you get it in your pocket? Is it
A gold or silver coin and
What could you buy with it?"

Had I asked something like that, the cat
Might have seen fit to blink
Or change the direction of its eyes,
As though it were *considering* the question,
While observing another galaxy…

I went into the garden late
And *could have sworn* it was an owl,
In fact it was a long, pale cat,
Bolt upright on the wall.

HOUSE MARTINS

At what time do the House Martins rise?

Definitely not before five…

I walked into the pale aftermath of dawn
To see not a single arrow-head of feathers
Swooping and darting under Heaven…
But go back half an hour later and

There they all are… … … … … !

As though they all rose as one,
"Come on! Time to check the River,
Time to welcome up the Sun."

MUST GO HOME

Cross faces are the finest things,
There's "nothing like" to cheer one up.
Hey! Is this another riddle or what?

Not exactly… well… I s'pose it is,
Here's the answer anyway:

When Eva, my one-of-twins twelve year old friend,
Goes all quiet, screws up her nose,
Very slightly clenches her teeth
And draws a veil across her eyes
To simulate veritably biblical thunder!
With all attendant lightning-strikes,
To show anger combined with part-feigned sorrow…

Simply because you've told her that
Mr. Tony regrets but
He really *has* to leave tomorrow.

> To show you care,
> No-one can say fairer.
>
> A cross face, as I was saying,
> Can be the finest thing.

CHARLIE BLUE

"Paint the back door blue," she said,
"I'll leave it up to you.
 Something like the colour it's now,
 Any old blue will do!"

I had a tin of "Cornflower," "Oxford..."
Plus shades from dark to light
And, in my box of oil paints,
Prussian, azure, cobalt...
"I'm the one who has to see it all day,
If it's all the same to you!
So, I think I should have a say,
If not be: THE ONE TO CHOOSE!"

I nearly jumped out of my skin,
I thought I was alone!
The voice came from behind, not far...
And somewhere down below, where
In a hutch, a rabbit lives, Charlie by name,
"That's right" he said "That door's my view,
I see it from my home.
It's my 'green fields' my 'vista,'
To gaze at when alone."

"That sounds reasonable to me,
 But should we stick to blue? You
 Might prefer" said I,
"another colour entirely?"

"No, blue is fine, it'll fit the bill, it'll
 Remind me of the sky,
 When the winter wind is cold and bleak,
 The air is full of frozen flakes
 And we're ALL wondering why...
 Let's not make it 'gloomy,'
 Like purple at funerals,
 On the other hand, not too 'nursery'
 Too 'baby' or 'boy blue' (little)..."

And as this conversation
Between Rabbit and Man went on,
It never occurred to me to say: "Wait
A sec… … … Hang on!"
So smooth and long were Charlie's words,
His voice of silk, soft as his ears,
If such things can exist in the World,
Then none of us need fear… … but
"Wake up Tone!" the rabbit added,
"This is no time to MUSE!
We're trying to find a colour and
YOU must help me choose…
The colour of a summer sky, with
With not a cloud to view, when
The yellow sun is riding high…
THAT'S the kind of blue.
So please unlatch and let me out,
Can't see at all from here!"
So he joined me at the mixing table
And folded back his ears… … …

Like Scientists or Wizards,
Or Leonardo da Vinci (the great),
We added a touch of rose madder,
Of turquoise, of violet.
I was amazed at his knowledge of colour,
Not once, not twice but thrice!
He may well have been a famous painter,
In a former life?

"And, just for fun, to give it an edge,
We put in a hint of Venetian Red,
Which is somewhere between autumn leaf
And the shades of Dragons' blood."

"What is the name of this colour?"
Asked the Lady of the House.
"It's a new one. It's 'Charlie Blue'" I said.
"One day it will be famous."

CONCENTRATE

[ON CENTER CAT]

Here's a bash at an animal fable,
About a cat, who, unobserved, was watching
A bird on a branch "just up there" and shall we say,
"accessible," savouring the action, the chase and the MEAL.
He made his move, quick and quiet as a snake but
Couldn't resist, on his way up the tree, sharpening
His claws to (as it were) make the pleasure complete.
This, of course, alerted the bird, which launched itself
Into the wind. The moral of this tale, I think you'll find:
We'll never get round to celebrate
Unless we WHOLLY concentrate!

GREAT SPOTTED or GREEN & DECKER

Mother Nature must have made
The Woodpecker just for fun.
I mean… why can't they forage for twigs
And build nests like all the other ones?
But thank the Lord for their clean as barrels,
Round as tinned–potato holes,
Drilled in the trunks of oak and fir
And across the dappled wood, their work,
Rattling like gunfire.

CATDREAM

They all dream of a special prize:
"Every seven hundred years, a cat will fly"
And chase one bird, for a while,
Up and down and round the sky.

So, when they make gigantic jumps,
Through necessity, or just for fun,
Out of madness, or one eye blind to fear,
Are they not thinking that I'M the one,
And THIS might be the year?

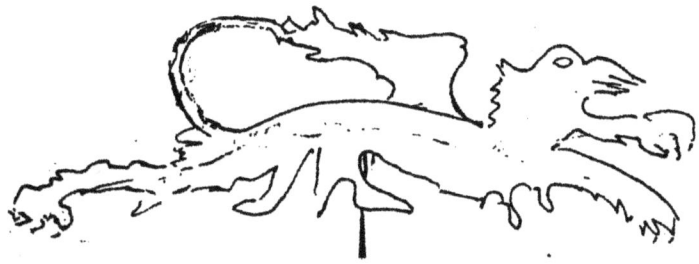

Weather-vane at Burg Greifenstein. Castle in the Hills of Hessen, Germany.

A RIVER WITH G

A poem for Gesa – her group of girls,
Playing intently, chewing pencils,
Who urgently asked me, so friendly and keen:

"A river with 'G' Tony… please… rack your brains…"

No luck! Not a thing!! mmmm? Danube with D,
Rhein with R… …Thames with T… …only LATER
Did a picture emerge of the gorgeous Guadalquivir,
That rides through Olive groves, Oranges, Almonds,
Desert and Meadow, the Stars and the Sun,
Stately and fine, a Queen indeed! through
Andalucia to the great Ocean.

Only later it came to me
And I was born in India!
Anyone got there? A huge,
Powerful, spiritual river…??
Rhymes with Camembert
              And Brie….

NO WEBS

FINAL OFFICIAL PROCLAMATION
To All Spider Population.

NO WEBS

Across the path that leads
Through the Buddleia and the Honeysuckle.

This also applies to the gap between
The Wild Rose and the Apple.

These are reserved solely for Humans.

BY ORDER - LANDLORD OF THE GARDEN.

And in the small print it says:

There are any *number* of shady places
Which are just as good to catch a fly,
Where the blackberry and the borage grow
Between the forgotten forget-me-nots
And the shiny green ivy you can
Weave away to your heart's content,
Quite undisturbed by listless giants,
Back from the pub, in search of the Moon
Or bleary-eyed in dressing-gowns
(or even nothing on), who couldn't sleep,
Wandering and wondering and blundering about
And woken up far too soon.

WITHOUT SURPRISE

For Ben

Here's a wise owl
for your birthday.
I think I saw him
on our walk in the deep forest.
He was asleep,
high in the branches
of the tallest pine tree,
waiting for the night
and dreaming of the poor mice
who would be his dinner
and of the moon,
who would light his way.

There flies a shadow, eyes like lasers,
Claws like steel and sharp as razors,
Feathers thick as castle walls,
No mercy, like a stone he falls.
He doesn't feel like you or me,
Cry or laugh or even worry—

To sail a silk-smooth August night
When silver stars shed silver light,
November when the frost comes brittle,
The forest's bones all creak and crackle,
Or Winter, when once grey wolves howled,
It's all the same to Mr. Owl.

Warm Spring days when buds are born,
Nature rubs her eyes, breaks free
Until the artist Autumn comes
And splashes gold on every tree.
Then his fantastic canvas done,
With his brush, paints out the sun.
Whatever season smiles or scowls,
It's all the same to Mr. Owl.

But maybe not...

One day at London Zoo,
I was waiting in the queue,
Hoping that the Kids weren't lost
I couldn't believe how much it cost,
I had to buy them funny hats
And then ice-cream on top of that,
I'm not that mean, don't get me wrong,
I just hoped the money'd gone
To buy the lions juicy bones
Or even get them tickets home—
A London lion's life's no joke
And I'm sure they'd love to see their folks...

We saw:

Tigers pacing nervously,
The gorilla's distant dignity,
Rats and snakes and other things
And lovely birds that didn't sing
But the ones who've stayed with me till now,
You've guessed it Ben, it was the Owls.
All day their deep eyes haunted me,
A road right back through History
To when man lived by Nature's Law,
His greatest fear... the Dinosaur?
And everything that's happened since—
Beggar, soldier, sage or prince
      They watch it all
                    Without surprise
    And that is why
                  We call owls wise.

MIDNIGHT FEAST

Kids can hide me
In the palms
Of their hands,
Like Anna:
Guitar-playing
Alice
In wonderland.

Sharp and shiny as a
Silver mirror,
Brittle as a witch's broomstick,
Tough and tenuous as a rose

So…

When my Dad asked,
Later that evening,
"What have you achieved…?"

I said,

"Here's a thing:

Got in a jam session
With Anna,

Two guitars
Chatting, whistling,
At one
O'clock
On a windy morning."

CHAPTER 3

THE ISLE OF EMERALD, RUBY AND RAINBOWS

IN A SAUCEPAN

In a saucepan, we caught a crab,
Observed and sketched it
Then let it go, but it wandered back as though
It liked us... White Strand, Co. Mayo,

And it only had five legs, we pondered,
Is this the way that crabs are made?
Or was it "boldly carrying on"
In the rough and tumble of the ocean?

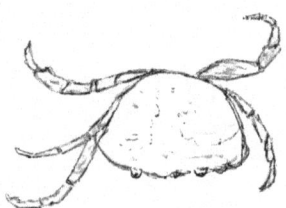

FAERY TALE, CONNEMARA

I came to Connemara
To seek the waters and the wild,
Battered but stoned from peddling songs
on the rocky roads of Ireland,
Who at this time seemed keen
to perpetuate her name as
A plasterer of the skies with grey
and purveyor of endless rain.

I dropped a dripping hitcher,
forlorn and on his own,
And I'd say he too was, tentatively,
praying for some sun,
And maybe he was thinking:

"Who'd leave home, to wander and roam
and be a lone hitch-hiker?"
as he stepped into a world spun with rain,
Like the webs of a million spiders.
I'd been given a kind of treasure map,
Like the ones you see in pirate stories:
"Land on Craggy Island, find the tree
struck by lightning, take ten paces
towards the hills," that kind of thing, Then:
Take the road for Connemara,
Turn left at Maam Cross,
or was it right? I couldn't remember,
(the map was only in my head,
The torn-off piece of yellowed parchment
had long since been lost)
So I turned... right,
nothing to choose between
Four roads airbrushed
into the sky by rain.

I came to a cosy–looking hotel,
Lounge at the back with open fire,
Four chairs ranged, all in a ring,

So I took one and waited for those
who I sensed would soon be coming...
Sure enough,
Three women and a golden child,
A boy of some four years,
The women, warm and smiling asked:
"O.K. if we sit here?"
I quoted Yeats and the smoke as it rose
and coiled from the dull turf–fire,
Swayed to the music of his words,
A Connemara cobra:

"Come away, O human child
To the waters and the wild,
With a faery hand in hand..."

But the child was worried, in the car,
he had six sleeping teddy-bears,
Were they all right? Were they lonely?
Locked in their sealed box of steel,
Were they cold? Were they worried themselves?
Were they still THERE?!
So his mum went out to investigate
And brought two of them in.
They sat on the floor, facing the fire,
Where they looked extremely comfortable,
And the boy grew happy and changed
From human child to, near enough, human angel.
"The Faeries would love this one,"
I said, just joking, to his mum...

And his mother took his hand
and drew him to her,
Put one arm round his waist,
the other tight under his chin,
Narrowed her eyes to a kind of smile
and said: "Well... they're not gettin' him."

And I felt a shiver pass through the room,
A mirror wrinkled like a rippling stream

And the curtains caught their breath and filled,
Like sails billowing in the wind.

"They're not gettin' him," she said,
As her two companions closed ranks,
Enfolded the boy in symbolic wings,
I thought: "God help any Faery,
Even Her Majesty herself, The Elfin Queen,
Who dared come near this human child
and his three guardian women."

...STREET DEAL

I call him the Bernard Shaw of the park bench–
For his long grey beard and steely bright eyes…
(Not so bright as Mr. Shaw's, but then, who has… ?!…)

After appraisal and forecast of the weather,
He asked if I had seventy pence, explained,
"I'm a bit short till Friday... till I get paid."

"There's fifty" I said
(being a bit short myself)
thinking this might suffice
or possibly be "Quite a good deal…"

Without aggression or even impatience,
Without a "please" or trace of embarrassment,
Perhaps knowing that my Maths had
Always been "a bit short" themselves!

"Another twenty" he said, and waited
Till I fished out a ten and then two fives,
As though he were a father kindly
Teaching a child how to handle money.

MONARCH OF THE ROOF–TOPS

Mediterranean weather
All over County Clare
And in the dark-blue evening,
Just before the stars,
The Blackbird sings across his kingdom,
From chimney-pot to grey stone tower.

Poulnabrone dolmen is a portal tomb in County Clare, Ireland

ENNIS SUMMER

"Swallow, swallow, little swallow, stay with me one night longer"
                              Oscar Wilde.

Two swallows on the gutter
Having their morning wash an' brush up, an'
Making quite a fuss!
With beak as comb and wing as duster—
In white waistcoats and wedding suits,
The main thing for a swallow's
To be well turned out.

Well… perhaps… not the main thing;
To look superb for them goes without saying,
But if we wish to know
The secrets of the little swallow
We simply have to
Get up CLOSE…

You won't believe
How you'll marvel
When you see
The details.

Get close enough to see them breathe,
Resplendent in their suits of satin,
With finest linen underneath
And to cap it all, they also wear
A rusty red handkerchief.

FIFTEEN MILES

Down by the graveyard, you're bound to see him
Pounding the roads around his home.
He was pointed out and I was told the tale
Of the man who walks fifteen miles a day.
Thus he covers, so to speak,
A vast distance every week,
Over four hundred miles a month,
The length of Ireland, or, from London,
[heading north]
Across the Borders into Scotland.

Might we not suggest he gets
a staff and spotted handkerchief
and that with a few possessions,
Instead of going round and round,
He goes on and on and on.

Think of the trees and streams he'd meet,
Not to mention the people!
The fields, forests, the ridges and Inns,
The rivers and the hills.

YEATS' TOWER

WHEN THE TRAVELLER DISCOVERS THAT THERE REALLY IS A TOWER — AND THAT IT WASN'T JUST A TITLE FOR A COLLECTION OF POEMS.

To Yeats' tower where fear of death
Beset him and I, out of breath
Arrived to find an open door,
Another piece for this jigsaw

To see his poem upon the wall
In this rhyme-scheme that is my model—
Invitation from the hand of chance
To carry on this tenuous dance.

KILSHEELAN BRIDGE*

On The River Suir, Co. Tipperary

Cill Siolan bridge in the evening sun,
The crumpled, lichened, wizened stone,
With a rippling rapid… just out there…
Playing the pan-pipes of the river.

But when the rapid's covered quite,
The river's full and fit and flat, it's
Under the vaulted arch of stone,
You'll have to go to hear the tune.

Here's to places of pilgrimage,
Which mirror the spirit and the divine,
Where there's usually water and foliage,
Always stillness… and very often stone.

*modern spelling

WROTE A CAROL FOR THE RADIO

Wrote a carol for the Radio—
A "Christmas Contest," full of hope,
We sent it off for interview.

Went through what it would say,
Time and again... What tone of voice,
What line it would take...

Scrubbed its face and brylcreamed its hair,
Clean underpants and socks and shined
its shoes so deep you could see
All the way to Australia...
Sent it off on the morning mail
with a hug and "good luck"
and packed lunch to Dublin...

As far as we know, it didn't
GET an interview. It sat,
Legs dangling on the waiting-room chair,
With all the others, many of whom,
were with broad-shouldered Dads
and Don't-mess-with-me Mums.

Well... needless to say, it didn't win
or even get given a spin on the air...
In short: it didn't get a look-in... So

We sent it off to Italy
and it found a job down there,
Translated and published in Italian,
Is happy for the moment living
in the just north of Venice sun,
(without even having to unpack its tune.)

Put not your faith in competitions
But don't stop writing
and keep on listenin', since

"There's a light in the sky tonight..."
Where is it leadin'? What is it saying?

SERIOUS RAIN

(The first few times I went to Ireland, I remember distinctly "the first pint." This time, it was just "A glass" (Irish for half-pint and with absolutely no "R" in the pronunciation) as I had a long, windy drive ahead... the breadth of the Land... with rain on the wind...)

The first glass, with Colin, hitchhiker,
English, and, HE said, World Traveller.
In Mullingar, due west of Dublin,
Festival on, street bunting, as the barman
Lined up our hollowed cones, our slender lilies
Of stout Guinness, plucked them from among the squad
Of broad shouldered and muscular pints—
The hobnailed boot and the delicate shoe
Sharing the same magical storm:
The frenzied downward thrusting bubbles,
As though, in the dark world of Faery,
The King had sounded the alarm…

Which echoed all the way to Sligo, when,
At the sign for Roscommon,
The serious rain began.

RECORDING THE SEA

(Inspired by a BBC Radio programme on J. M. Synge)

Holding a mic.
to the mouths of the waves

a matchstick
figure on the beach.

Delegation
from the upstart world
of Radio
and electronics.

Chapter 3 - "The Isle of Emerald, Rudy and Rainbows"

TO IRELAND

In the queue for the boat to Dublin—"DELAYED ONE HOUR"—
It does seem, when coming to Ireland there's always SOMETHING...
Not to mention "Slatterys," the coach firm
that guarantees, let's just say, "Adventure."

> *But realised suddenly what it is*
> *about Long Red Hair...*
> *A girl has just walked past with,*
> *Hanging round her shoulders*
> *A waterfall of fire.*

~~~~~~~

"There was once a coach firm called CLATTERYS,"
With orange letters and two green stripes
And the drivers were all Frontier Scouts,
With nicknames like Carson and Crockett and Boone
And the reins which drove six green horses
were loose and largely urging them on.

I first encountered one of their Stages
on the rocky road to Fishguard, Wales,
In gloomy mood, sulky and sour.
Twisting and turning, making my way
To the boat that leaves in the darkest hour...
(half three in the morning — just before dawn)

When SUDDENLY, beside me appeared:
A ramshackle palace on wheels,
Out of nowhere it seemed to come,
Through the mist, riding the storm:
A brightly coloured Ship of Fools—
Up on the verge, stones flying,
Tilted at 45 degrees, then swallowed
by the hole bored in the night
by my Ford Cortina's headlights and the DRIVER,
Who I didn't see, but IMAGINED (and
later found I was right), had:
Stetson flying out behind, locks
Stretched and curling in the wind,

Lashing on his foaming team
Proud to be part of the Clattery Game.

So THAT'S the way, I realised,
The inexpensive option:
For The Broke... The Daily Grind,
The Local Bus to Ireland.

The "Clattery's Bus" – no frills no bull
Conveyor of bags and Sunday suits,
Nun's habit and cloth cap,
Backpack and slung guitar,
Books of songs from Streets of London
To Athenry and the Wild Rover,
Hairy legs and torn jeans
Accents from "birrrminham" to "austrailian..."

Wrap it all up at Victoria Station
Send it spinning "o'er" hill and dale
The ancient Ridgeway, the Severn Valley
Into and beyond the pale.

Once I heard a little girl, who'd thrown up twice
but now settled down to singing the Hokey Cokey
Over and over again... Hoookey... Cokey
Hooooookey... Cokey... interspersed with: "Everybody..!
C'mon... I can't hear ya'... That's better...
Even louder!... That's loud enough!!
Her small voice kept, those awake, in thrall,
A routine she'd heard at a wedding or dance-hall
As the bus snored, headed West to Mecca,
By now, well under the Faeries' spell,
As it buzzed and rattled and nosed its way
To the ocean
Past Laugharne (pronounced Larne)
where I, at least, waved to Dylan,
Then on by sleeping towns and hamlets—
the road that runs through the land of Merlin.

Clattery's Bus, no frills, no bull...

That reminds me of a tale. Let me just say:
Before my Dad died he said to me, not
"To thine own self be true" or "Play
up, play up and play the game!" These
are things he'd already covered...
Things we'd both been through...
and he didn't use the words "My son"
(perhaps he did between the lines)
But he did say "Tone, whatever you do,
Tell the World the Clattery's Story
Just the way you told it to me."

In fact, the very first time
I decided to leave the car
and chance my arm... Nothing but
Sagas of woe had I heard:
The Clattery's Bus... Oh my God!!

So I took my courage in both my hands
Girded, as it were, tightly my loins and
JUST MANAGED... to get a ticket in time.

One hour's shuffling in the queue
Kicking, dribbling my bag and guitar case,
Emerging triumphant into the sun, to see
FOUR Clattery's buses (no less).

Into the sun with a ticket for Ireland,
Through this land of Europe to the end of the West,
But you'll have to wait for the second book if
You want to hear the rest...

THE ISLE OF EMERALD, RUBY AND...

NOT TO MENTION *THE WEATHER* IN THE WEST:
A lot of the time you can't see the place!
Due to mist and rain and tyre-spray
And when you can, it's all "ups and downs,"
Cider-brown streams, lop-sided hawthorns,
Gorse bushes, salty winds, marshes and stones.

IRELAND — BY ANY OTHER NAME
As for the title: "Emerald Isle,"
It is "green," yes, it can't be denied,
But in view of the Fuchsia and the berries:
The Hawthorn, the Rose-hip, The Rowan and Holly,
Might we not amend and say:
The Isle of Emerald and Ruby?
But come to think, when bringing up
This important question of "colour,"
Bearing in mind the variety, the
Sudden and continuous changes in weather,
How rain and blue sky can ebb and flow
[All seasons bundled into an hour]
Might we not extend and say:
The Isle of Emerald, Ruby and Rainbows?

BRONZE, STONE AND PATHS TO THE SUN. Ancient Ireland, before
The Celts came.

A LANGUAGE WOVEN FROM SILVER AND FIRE. The Irish language,
an eagle's eye view. E.g. The poetry of Women's Names:
Niambh, Cliodhna, Aoife, Siobhan
Pronounced: Nieve, Cleeonah, Eefa(Eva), Schivorn.

ALL NIGHT STORY

The river normally wending its way
Round the rocks and between the ferns,
Was now in a frenzy… FURIOUS!
In the night, it had grown
And become a monster with wild-horse manes
Curling and thrashing dragons' tails,
Utterly ignoring its appointed path,
The stones it skirts — the wall it shoulders…

Woken in the middle of the night, it seemed
Someone was throwing handfuls of grain
At the window, so hard was the wind
And the water flying around
And after the sun was well–up at nine,
In dark sheets over the tarmac rushing...
The storm was *still going*! The rain,
Hot-foot from the top of the town,
At the cross-roads... ...
Had to make up its mind
To head west or south
But to *carry on down!*

And on the morrow the stream was still
Bubbling and boiling but infinitely calmer,
It had returned, more or less,
To its everyday, tinged with brown,
Old, reliable, cider–press–river.

ON TOUR IN ULSTER

Through the road-block, R.U.C. men
flat-capped, bullet-proofed.
Garish paintings grace the buildings,
Pavement to roof –
Militant frescoes spill their message
like the bad King James's blood,
depicted here, pierced to the heart
by a regal Orange sword

King William's charger, in execution
hardly worthy of a child's pen –
Three figures, lifeless, wooden, dead-pan,
sinister....

Next door a plaque:

> "In Memory of...
> Murdered by
> The Enemies of Ulster"

on every house a Union Jack
or George's Cross

"Vita – Veritas – Victa."

And what I'd come to do
was to seek a shop called Paragon
(well-known ladies haberdasher)
and for her bonny red hair to buy
some green and silken ribbon.

But try the other side of town,
See the competition:
The brushwork on the bricks, their street illustrations:
No piping, finery, fairy-tale images of Kings
but masked men, hooded ravens,
brandishing the gun.

Spent days here at my own road block:
How to end this poem?
Round it off, wind it up, reach a neat conclusion,
And the kids in the schools I played were also keen
to find a solution.

So,
Come Ye with swords and Ye with guns
and Us, with words and good intentions,

Any suggestions?   Any suggestions?

Written in 1991 while performing and playing in Ulster

COMEDY OF MANNERS

Derry woman, Mum, knocked about
by a war-zone life. Warm,
Sceptical, powerful shoulders,
Came round to visit with her son...

A lad of few words and low-flying eyes,
Hair close shorn, a bale of straw,
A jagged, raggy, sabre–slashed mop,
A jumbled handful of Bridget's Crosses...

We offered them both a cup of tea,
''No'' he said, edgy, still hedge-hoppin',

"No WHAT!" said his mum...

In the silence that ensued,
The stillness after the thunder clap,
His eyes became an alligator's,
Wily, beady, sending feelers
Into all departments of his brain.
Here was somewhere to sink his teeth:
"No WHAT!" What could she mean??

But having found no solution,
On the count of four,
His answer came:

(two)

(three)

(four)

"No... ... ... tea?"

CHAPTER 4

MERRIE ENGLAND

GREEN AND PLEASANT LAND

ANOTHER RIVER SONG*

Through the Hampshire hills and hop–fields green
Runs a river called the Wey
And it would keep me company, well, me and my bike
When there was nothing to do that day
And like the rippling river I would sing: "You know
I flow therefore I am."
And I felt I shared the freedom of the dragon-flies
And the strength of the Coulee Dam

So won't you flow sweet river, flow down to the sea,
With your wandering weeds and bubbling beads philosophy,
Run sweet river, run down to the sea,
Polish your stones and whistle your tunes and take it easy.

And on winter days I would go my ways
When the iron earth was still
And winter's jagged cloak of white
Lay quiet on the hills
And the only ones who seemed to carry on
Were the ghostly heron tall
And the rooks and man and the river spun
Through icy waterfalls
We were waiting for the spring
The laying-on of the swallows' wings
And the life that the sun would bring
To stretch our throats and sing... ...

Won't you flow sweet river, flow down to the sea,
With your wandering weeds and bubbling beads philosophy,
Run sweet river, run down to the sea,
Polish your stones and whistle your tunes and take it easy.

Song from, "The Cypress, The Hemlock, The Flowers and The Vine" 1980.

AUTUMN

Early fog-patches across Wales will have dispersed by late morning."
That's the forecast for today—the 13th October—BBC Radio Three.

Autumn — What I always loved!
No frost yet but that
Old familiar chill, that
Freshness, that brittle purity.
No tawdry frills, no flies but
If you look carefully:
Hedge-spiders webs "all dew"
And the deep, dark red
Of the hawthorn berry
Shining,
Like new.

STANDING STONE – CORNWALL – FOURTH CENTURY A.D.

So where IS this stone?? All the guide book said:
It stands in the village of Whitecross,
One and a half miles from Wadebridge,
Somewhat to the south of the A39.

When I got there, I asked all visible locals
And all of them, sorry, hadn't a clue, till
I found a bloke in a council van,
Munching sandwiches on his own,
"I'm naat from roun' 'ere," he said,
"Sorry mate... ... ...I wouldn' know...
But I've got a maap, troi tha' if you like."

Sure enough, miles from where I'd imagined,
Was a little drawing, way off the road,
Down a track from a Y–Junction,
Captioned with the words: "Inscribed Stone."

Thought it might be a trigpoint or nipple,
Crowning some brazen, moorland hill, in fact
It's protected by two ancient cedars,
By a pink house with a silver slate roof,
A tiered garden with interesting shrubs
And a propped–up Polo millstone, also:
A beige oriental cat
with pale blue eyes and a gruff face,
whose job it is
To check–out strangers.

ELY CATHEDRAL

Came on the feast of Candlemas,
as last year, to the day,
To look this time, not just drink in,
So... What did I see?

I saw the myriad pipes of the organ,
Some it seemed as small and thin
as descant recorders,
all in gold, entwined, veined
with rich, dark colours.

I saw… Sepulchres:
Massive tombs of bishops, honeycombed
with bone–sharp–shouldered mandalas,
in pale grey crumbling stone:
"John Barnett — Bishop of Ely, 1366 to '73,"
And heraldic shields, heart-shaped, deep red,
Midnight blue, overlaid with Fleur de Lys,
Triple crown, Cross Keys, Sacred Heart and
crudely painted wounded hands and feet.

I saw... the carving
in a small chapel (Bishop West's 1515),
He came from Putney, son of a baker,
Maybe explains why the stonework
is as over–the–top and detailed
as the proverbial wedding cake,

And on the ceiling, cherub faces,
plump-cheeked, sinister dolls,
and, to boot, what seemed a host
of Green Men in leaf apparel
(I could just pick out their faces
as the night began to fall):
Jack in the Green
They used to call him,
Where wood and bone become one,
Or Jack in the Bush!

Out of his mouth, curving branches
like a thick moustache......
Jack in the Bush,
Half tree, Half man,
Lord of the Woods and Joy of Woman,
Jack in the Bush, Jack in the Green,
What on earth can he be doing,
Cheek by jowl with The Holy Virgin?

In...
in this place which has breasted wind and sun,

Stood firm
Nine hundred years in oak and stone,

Dressed up for
Christmas, Candlemas, all manner
of celebrations.

Looked down on
Hallowe'en and gazed with envy at Mayday
Dancing on the Village Green.

Played host
to Pedlar, Peasant, Knight,
Saint, Beggar, King and Queen.

Built
almost on water, with incalculable vision then,
Now, a beacon for all to see
        for miles
                across The Fens.

THE FIVE SISTERS WINDOW

"No words can describe it; it must be seen."
    H. V. Morton

A work of extraordinary...
.... intricacy.
Five lofty columns of glass,
A gentle darkness at their core.
A host of medieval mandalas,
Flecked with flashing colour:
Red... yellow... blue...
A vast and delicate web of lead
Split by shafts of stone. Like
Gun-metal images of the moon
With flames
            darting through.

The Five Sisters window dominates the north transept of York Minster, York, England.

THERE WAS A TIME BEFORE THE TV

There was a time before the TV,
Before the radio,
When music only came from the fingers
From the heart and from the throat.
There was a time when the players came
And the whole town fell in thrall,
I ain't sayin' things were better then,
I ain't sayin' that at all.

There was a time when the thunder roared,
You'd reach out for a hand,
When every storm meant something,
Like the raven and the wind.
The oak tree was shelter, the holly joy
And the rain came through the walls,
I ain't saying things were better then,
I ain't saying that at all.

HACKPEN HILL–AVEBURY

The horses on Hackpen-three white, the other black
Apart from one scratched in the chalk,
Who welcomes those who face the hill,
To the soul and spirit of Equus.

We saw them first in silhouette,
(Figures in a Magic Lantern)
Against the sky while evening fell,
As we climbed the steep flank of Hackpen
(means Head of the Serpent, from times long gone) and
We couldn't possibly have known then but that moment
They'd been set free! When we got to the top, the
Horse-box was there, engine still running
And their keepers were standing, watching… So
No wonder they were prancing so fine,
Heads high and manes shaking
(Apocalyptic beasts from the fold, unchained
On a green hill far away)
Looking at everything and nothing!
Casual, enraptured, let loose, released,
Checking out the possibilities
And the borders of being free.

THE ROLLRIGHT STONES

I cannot go to The Rollright Stones,
(a circle on the Banbury Downs)
observe their shape, read the blurb
and coolly go my way. No! I have to listen
to the wind and find out where in
the year's cycle, the local Hawthorn stands
and in the knowledge that the King Stone
was once taken down to the river
to be used as a bridge — it
took twenty horses to drag it there,
down the steep slope to the stream,
and when the job was done, as though
it couldn't wait to get back Home,
They hauled it up with one.

So, as I say, I have to retrace,
all the way down to the water,
just as the story tells,
then walk back up with the solitary horse
to be part of the miracle.

SPELSBURY CHURCH

By a primitive, tin money-box, in Olde Worlde script was written:

"𝔓𝔦𝔩𝔤𝔯𝔦𝔪 𝔭𝔩𝔢𝔞𝔰𝔢 𝔰𝔭𝔞𝔯𝔢 𝔞𝔫 𝔬𝔣𝔣𝔢𝔯𝔦𝔫𝔤 𝔱𝔬 𝔥𝔢𝔩𝔭 𝔴𝔦𝔱𝔥 𝔱𝔥𝔢 𝔲𝔭𝔨𝔢𝔢𝔭 𝔬𝔣 𝔱𝔥𝔦𝔰 𝔞𝔫𝔠𝔦𝔢𝔫𝔱 𝔠𝔥𝔲𝔯𝔠𝔥."

Please find my:

DONATION WITHIN

[Silver Coin]

For The Lady with The Unicorn and
For her Heron, patient, stately.
For the tattered White Ensign, high in the rafters,
At peace now, far from the sea.
For the jigsaw pieces of Norman stone.
For the Silence... ...and for the Door Open...

And for recognizing those who roam
by calling me a Pilgrim.

[Which, incidentally I was and am]   I come...
I came from the fields,
A pacing scarecrow,
Following the paths and the bridleways,
With no idea where I'd left the car,
Footloose now in Paradise.

And I saw, close-up, a Kingfisher,
Caught unawares by still water,
As I wandered aimless… but, trust me!
To land in a place called Spelsbury.

Having previously met a Heron,
Rising on broken umbrella wings
Flapping a pace across the pond
And parachuting into the reeds.

I played my recorder to some swans,
Who made me distinctly un-welcome
But nevertheless, I played them a tune:
"The Holly and The Ivy" to be polite
and recognize their home.

And then, despite their unconcern,
I recited them a rhyme:

>"Had I not become a man,
>I might as well have been a swan,
>Living happy ever after
>Between the river and the stars."

And continued with a riddle then,
Which I'd mainly based on them:

"I change my clothes once a lifetime??" [Who am I?]

No reply!

Before moving on.

FOR THE SPELSBURY CHILDREN

Little tin box with a slit for a coin
And a keyhole, so battered and bent,
What kind of key could possibly fit?!
One of chocolate perhaps, or peppermint?

Does it live on the Vicar's jangling ring?
Must you put it in from a particular angle?
Is it deep in a pocket or secretly hanging?
Or simply kept by an Angel?
Who opens the box, in fact, by magic—
Doesn't need a key at all!?

All these thoughts went through my mind,
As I heard the silver coin fall,
In the silent church, no other sound
But the passing of time and the whispering wind.

GIG AT FROYLE MILL

At the third rich seam I found
(of blackberries),
A herd of cows in the neighbouring field
gathered round to watch me.

When I'd finished
and my plastic bag
bubbled with purple fruit,
I sang them a song
about the madness of war
and the beauty of a flower
in a woman's hair,
to thank them
for their support.

Then the ones who'd shunned
my run-of-the-mill performance
as a picker,
came with haste
from the far corners of the field
to join their sisters—

mainly I s'pose to find out
what on earth was going on
and to examine
what must have been for them
a curious phenomenon,

as I made the Hills of Hampshire ring,
the cows gazed silently
and their mournful eyes
watched my fingers
strum the ukulele...

"I dreamed about a rose in a Spanish Garden,
and I kiss you as I place it in your hair.
If I'm ever on my feet again, I will,
I will run all the way just to meet you there!"*

* *Lyrics from the song "Last letter home" by David "Butch" McDade/James. H. Brown Jr.*

THE PEDDARS WAY*

As I roved out one morning,
In the autumn of the year,
With a dark night snapping at my heels...,
And all night long the jewelled sky,
A bitter wind swept clean
As she blew like a train across the fields.
The road that I was walking,
Had been there two thousand years
And a thousand years before that there it lay...,
And the wind hung in the hawthorn
And the birds did sing,
As the sun gleamed on the Peddars Way.

Well sometimes I get the notion
That I've got to hit the road,
So I hit the oldest road in the land
With the ages of man gazing down from the trees,
I heard footprints in the air, sounds in the sand.
Though she was flying right behind me all along the day,
I was going to tell her every detail, every line;
So I carved them in paper, drew diagrams in stone
And stored it all like jewels in my mind.

And as I came to the Holy Land of Blessed Walsingham
Four daughters of the church I chanced to meet—
With their hoods of blue and their faces scrubbed,
And all of seventeen,
White socks and brown sandals on their feet
And they looked at me as though I was
The False Knight on the road,
As though I'd sprung from the hedgerow like the Fiend!
As we talked, we saw the light,
Theirs was shining for the Lord
And mine was far across the sea.

I've seen the ruins of the Forum,
I've seen ruins in the East,
I've seen ruins of great beauty in this land.

I've seen ruined homes and palaces,
But I have never seen
Ruins like the ruins of Walsingham.
The foliage behind them of the deepest elfin green,
With no knowledge of Christ's blood – the iron nails,
And as white birds flew around
The honey arched stone,
I swear I saw the Grail.
With the wind still in the hawthorn,
But the birds had ceased to sing,
As the sun set on the Peddars Way.

* The opening track of Tony Maude's album "Almost True" 1982.

MERRIE ENGLAND

LONDON BRANCH

CHRISTMAS CHEER IN DRYBURGH ROAD, PUTNEY

For John Betjeman

Loading bricks in Dryburgh Road,
Winter, as English winters go —
Damp December, darkened leaves
Lined the pavement and the street.
I was listening to the radio...

Turned up, full volume, in the van,
To ease the work do what you can—
Doors open to the afternoon
Sweet music, make the job end soon—
What a sound and what a band.

A woman from a house nearby
Approached, no need to wonder why,
I searched her face, assumed a frown,
Well, if she asks, I'll turn it down—
I'd hoped to get the whole street high.

But till she speaks, I'll stand my ground
Transfixed, elated by the sound
Of trumpets, choir and timpani
Joined in joyous harmony—
MUSIC makes the world go round.

"Who wrote this music, do you know?"
I shook my head... "so and so?"
"Could be, all I can say... sublime."
We stood and listened for some time
To Bach's Christmas Oratorio.

WHIRLIGIG

Frost again, in fact ICE!
A brittle skin on every pail,
A shiny coat on every car
And this is London… Imagine!
On a ploughed hill, with not a soul,
How one would feel
The spinning of the seasons.

DALMATIAN

As I went for a lone, kerb–kicking stroll last night,
round eleven in the spring–breeze air,
I saw what I thought was a piece of paper
Floating, cruising at roof height, along Deodar Road.
Cool, regal, firm, determined, almost majestic in its progress.
However, on closer and better–lit inspection,
It turned out to be not paper at all but an air–borne
DALMATIAN.

Which gracefully landed against some railings
By the arch that leads into the Park.
When I touched it, it rose again,
Heading for the river, the trees and the green,
For which, for some reason, the gate was still open. So,
With not a soul in Wandsworth Park, round midnight
I took the dog for a walk. He rose and hovered and carried on,
This life–size, gravity–defying balloon,
And then it followed me home.

I tied it to the washing–line and there it can stay for a while,
Until I can find a child or friend with whom I can
...ceremoniously launch it...
and re–release it to the wind.

LONDON THUNDER

From the upstairs window at Midnight,
Mesmerized by the storm, I saw
The Mum opposite open the door,
Look anxiously along the street...
I thought: "Oh dear, the teen—
age daughter has over-stayed, she'll
be in trouble, coming home late!"

Worry compounded by the thunder,
which was raging and the rain
was rivers in the gutters
and battering the pavements.

No sign...! but then!!
From the other way, came
the Dad and younger daughter,
Ambling... hand in hand, no coats,
Totally soaked and smiling.

The girl went in, to "relieved Mum!"
But Dad remained outside, in thrall,
Held-tight in the bosom of the storm.

A minute later, the same daughter,
poked her head through the open door,
All dry by now in dressing–gown: "Dad,
Dad, whataya doin'?!!" But answer came from Dad no word,
...On another continent, in another
Universe, how, indeed, would he have heard? There
He stood, arms outstretched to welcome in, be over—
whelmed by the rain. Head back—Eyes closed—
        At One.

"ROLL of HONOUR" for TWO WORLD WARS ONE PAGE TURNED EVERY DAY

Truman, Trussell,
Tucker, Tumber,
Turner, Turtle,
Tydeman, Tye,
Tyler, Tyrrell,
Tabor… so it went on
…to Valentine.
Just strange that on Feb. Fifteen,
Valentine should be there beside his brothers:
The last of the T's – What those guys,
Those "lads" must have suffered,
All that frozen, fear and rain
That Valentine made it, the day after,
I know will be forgiven.

It was a pleasure and a privilege
To meet them, I think they'd appreciate
The joke …the co-incidence I noticed,
"Oi! Valentine you're Late!"
strolling one Winter's morning into
St. Botolph's–without–Bishopsgate. *

---

* *Wren church, originally built in 1212 outside the ancient walls of the City of London, then! Now, just along the road from Liverpool Street Station.*

NEW NEIGHBOURS

The Squatters moved in quietly,
Under cover of night—
No-one knew until next day we
Saw their faded, make–shift curtains
And after dark, in the upstairs rooms
The flicker of candle light.

NO TIME

Today I saw you, late as usual,
Forcing your way along the street, as though
Against a wind… In fact it was a still, bright day,
The kind that ushers in the Spring. My cheerful blast on the horn
Took you by surprise. You had no time
To summon up your world–embracing smile,
To hide the jostling shadows that
Flickered in your eyes.

RUN OF THE MILL

What's your job? Don't ask me!
Day after day after day,
I work on the river and the
River works on me.

Only when the stream is frozen
And the Summer's half a world away...
Only when the river freezes am I
Free to take a holiday.

When the great timber wheel is locked
And the surface of the stream completely still,
Then I have the chance to wander,
Then I have the chance to travel

So that when the Spring and Summer come,
I too will have some tales to tell
The swallows and the roses, of Winter when
The river is a silver road,
When all the mills are frozen stiff
And hung with icicles…

Run of the mill they call me.
Run of the mill's my name.
It was a run of the mill life I led
Before the Winter came.

CHAPTER 5

THE ROAD, THE SHOW AND "THE MUSIC."

"Never so happy as when planning a journey."

IF ALL THE MUSIC…

If all the music were hoovered up,
The whole world would suddenly stop.

If all the paintings were blotted out,
Windows would cease to let in light.

If all the poems were collected and burned,
In a way, that would be the end.

If all the books were drowned or wiped…

We'd have to hide paintings behind the eyes,
Stored beside the tanks of tears.
Music and songs on shelves along
The tubes that run from the soul to the ears,
And poems jogging down the track
From the heart to the mind to the tongue and back.

I would become "Wuthering Heights,"
Good friend of "Great Expectations,"
Sharing a flat with "Mill on the Floss,"
"Heart of Darkness" and "Tess
Of the D'Urbevilles…"

Chapter 5 - The Road, The Show and "The Music."

A GIG

The phone rang...   with:
A Gig!
the whole room rang, with
A GIG!
The skies of London
RANG WITH A GIG...

Berwick–on–Tweed... ...mmmm...?
FIFTY-FIVE QUID!!

When I do this on stage as part of a comedy spot, I shade my eyes and gaze forlornly across four hundred miles in a northerly direction... before I deliver the mournful punch-line.

THE POETRY FESTIVAL

For Noelle

Arriving at night, we went straight to a pint
And our performance at The Best Hotel
In Killybegs, out on a limb,
On the shin of Donegal.

It wasn't till after mid-night that
We got to the house where we were staying...
"Shhh! There's someone asleep!" Taking a break,
An early night, from peddling poems
And revelling all week.

So we put the harp and guitar away
And had a whispered cup of tea.

The next morning we were up first, the
Sleeper we mentioned, still miles away...
As we awaited the kettle, I played a little
And watched the West of Ireland rain. When

The sleeper came down, himself a poet,
Weather-beaten and well-known, he had a kind of
Radiant expression... pointed to the harp,
Still wrapped in its blanket and said:
"I thought I'd woken up in Heaven!"

He said "The harp... I heard the harp playing,
I didn't know anyone was here... I thought
I'd woken up 'up there!'"

But the harp was where it had been all night,
Had not stirred... had not spoken... then
Gradually the penny dropped, the truth dawned,
Sesamé opened! There'd been no harp, no radio on,
The Heavenly Music had emanated from me, my
Fingers and the littl' ukulele! I played a cadence to demonstrate,

"Yes, that could have been ...that was it!" Look,
I only brought this story up, I

> Only tell this tale
> To show that once anyway
> I must have
> Played like an angel.

THE MUSIC

I often take the Uke about
With cosy case and shoulder–strap,
It's so convenient and compact,
One might as well as not…

'Twas in a small West Irish Town
By the choppy stone sea of The Burren,
We went into an Ale–House, just to
Check it out…

At the door we stood aside
For a little fellah on his way,
Distant eyes and reddish face, who
When he saw the instrument case,
Of a sudden came to life,
Clicked into focus.

At the simple presence of pipe or box
To blow or bow, pluck or pick,
Deadly serious to my eye said:
"Are you The Music?"

As though The Music roams the land
Like a King or Spirit in disguise
And may appear, regale, delight
Any where and any time!
This is its job, its duty and
He wasn't wrong of course,
In Ireland as no–where else I've seen
This is, more or less, the case!

So, what a privilege, a gas,
What a feather in one's cap,
Sigh no more, buck up, be glad
That by the Good Lord we've been picked
To be neither General nor Politician,
But what "your man" called "The Music."

MEDIEVAL MUSIC – HANOVER STATION

Dusty cloaks of russet, red and green,
Rusty locks of ginger, blonde and brown.
He played the pipes, she played the drum
and a mandolin underlined the rhythm,
Sitting, cross–legged on the ground.

A passionate, impromptu show, one
Winter's afternoon – for us, the
Match-stick men and women
That huddle round a teeming station.
The Winos, the Nutters and the "normal" people.
The usual crew of lost and busy souls.

The crumhorn reared its cobra head,
The crowd rained silver on their cymbal,
She stamped her feet to the thundering drum
and bells jangled at her heels…
Her half–closed eyes, with fiery smile
Were cocked to shoot your heart away,
Twist the knife that aches and longs
To cut us all free.
Forsake the feather–bed and fitted kitchen
and travel… … … … …with The Gypsies.

GERMAN FAIRY-TALE WINTER TOUR

Title inspired by Heinrich Heine's: Deutschland - Ein Wintermaerchen (Germany – a Winter's Fairy Tale). The story of his return home from exile in France.

In plenty of time, arrive Dover,
with confidence at last in overhauled carburettor.
About to drive into "wind's tail,"
As Eliot says: "forever bailing."

ON THE BOAT:

Dozed off in a moonlit glade,
Under a plastic pale–blue light, in this
almost empty, shut-down Disco, (a shabby,
abandoned fairground) I managed
to sleep for an hour or so...

ON THE ROAD:

Spires of Belgian churches
Gleaming like rapiers,
Delicate foils to
Our sturdy stone towers...

But all built to the glory of God,
To pierce the sky of every season.
Difficult resting place for snow, long
Shadow–makers for the sun.

GERMANY:

Slipped off the autobahn through fields of frost,
A winding road down to the river
And feeling fairly alone, I sang,
By the parked car, into the twilight:
"Joy, Health, Love and Peace,
Be all here in this place..."
Just for fun and to hear a voice, then
Came across a gingerbread town,

Chapter 5 - The Road, The Show and "The Music."

Timbered houses, tiny windows,
On the steep banks of the Rhine.
Bronze towers of floodlit castles
(shades of Siegfried and Brunhilde)
Stuck to the sleeping vineyard hills
Above the black–ink glinting water.

Stop for a long–awaited beer:
"Zum Rosenhof" (not far from Bingen),
Phone Laura, phoned Marianne,
No reply... ... No connection...

BAVARIA:

Woke up, it was a Moosburg morning
and everything in sight
had been dusted with snow.
It began last night when I left the pub,
Flecking the cars and the cobble stones,
In the wee small hours, not a soul...
Even the furrygreen, seasonal stars
Had been turned off, tucked up for the night
But the Christmas tree at the crossroads was still
studded with traditional white and the
Twin towers of Moosburg Church, magnificent
and gleaming in the half–light.

With Santa Maria, stone and wan,
Silent above the sleeping town,
Slender arm raised in blessing
Above the dangerous T–junction.

The Chemist, The Baker, all fast asleep,
Even, it seemed The Police Station,
But back in the Pub, a drinker had beckoned:
"Come hither and hearken to my tale,
Lend an ear to my dreams and troubles..."
But I left... for the wheel of an old English car,
Now rattlesnaking over the cobbles...

...sitting here now at a Bavarian table,
By box of string and shiny ribbon,
Out of the cupboard, about to spring
into Christmas decorations.
Snow falling fast, half–decent flakes,
Me, "Living on the breath of a song,"*
Planning a journey, map open... No
body much came last night,
Apart from my fans here,
ALL FIVE...

Couple of girls just "chatted" past,
Snow settling into their knotted scarves...

Last night, not knowing where I was,
I breathed out over a frozen lake,
Watched the steam... roll over the ice,
Then drove to work down frosty roads,
Lined with solemn spruce.

---

*"Living on the Breath of a Song," was written for me by Nigel Cameron—a wonderful song-writer—who died some years ago. The song has also "gone" – returned to the ether whence it came. If any of ye come across it, please send me a copy.

CHAPTER 6

THE WHOLE BUSINESS... OF POETRY

PRESENTATION

Poems should be spun with lights and pictures,
Danced and sung with the skill of the actor,
Fondled and dandled on the tongue…

They should not be handed, as a package
Bundled into the listeners' arms,
But unwrapped slowly, tastefully lit,
If you like use props or mime,
Even a touch of dry ice…

This is the way we should present them,
In this way we should let them loose…

Like a glider, launch them
Into the wind from the top of a hill,
Or through the laughter and the smoke
Like darts on their journey to the Bull…

One way or another, I suggest
We should get them into the air,
So the secrets the poems hold
Can be told, so to speak, in fire.

POETS

Poets are an awful pest, best
To keep well clear — They'll
Get you up against the wall and pour
Their ravings in your ear.
Desperate for an audience,
They'll raid you like a fridge,
If you so much as hint you like
John Donne or "...Upon Westminster Bridge."
They'll very quickly suss you out
And sidle round the room,
Within seconds, metaphorically,
They'll have one hand on your bum
And in the other, their very soul,
Their raison d'être, their POEM! So

Treat them nicely as you can
And really try to listen,
But leave your keys in the ignition,
Make sure you keep your exit clear,
And the front door
Firmly open.

TREASURER

of the local Poetry Society

There's no membership fee
And it's free to get in,
So how can he be Treasurer?
I'm sorry but I don't understand,
How can he have a viable job
When no money changes hands?

What is he, Mr. Clever–Clever?
A Treasurer without treasure?!
What does he lock in his little cash–box?
What does he cook in his cash–book?

I'm sorry if these questions appear
Somewhat dense, unless he's a Treasurer
In the sense of showing someone a shell
From the sea and telling them
How to hold it against their ear.
How to rustle a tambourine
Or tilt a rainmaker?

Is he a kind of Forest Ranger
Who takes people into the Wild?
Shows them where the poems are
And with a finger to his lips, whispers:
"Shssshh...! They're down there...!"

And, sure enough,
In the glade by the stream,
There's a green and gold snake
And a pale–blue swan
And in the early–morning mist,
Will come the Unicorns…

If he's a Treasurer along these lines, then
I rest my case... sorry… everything's fine.

PENCIL

Scribbling with this commandeered pencil
Which once was used to stir blue paint
And which I rescued from the shed
And a shadowy life in a cocoa tin
As a washing-line post for dust
H
   u   g
      n

on disused spiders' webs...

The blue paint thickly covers
To well over half way down—
A hooded cloak wrapped tight,
Up to and beyond the chin.
How's that for a mask, if ever there was one?!:

No HB, no STAEDLER, no COUNTRY OF ORIGIN,
Not a trace whence this stranger came—
The time-honoured and eternal pencil,
Waiting to be taken along the road—

And this is what the pencil said:

"Come on, let's stride the straight and narrow, go
Up and down the winding ways...

Let me help you to express.

I can help you to explain."

TO DRAW OR NOT TO DRAW

A bit like
Crossing a river on stepping–stones,
Or spelling a
Long and difficult word. One
Weighs up the risks
And chances of success;
Summons up the courage, the skill and the wit,
And either "thinks better" and turns away
Or steels oneself and goes for it.

Three ravens on a coin. Bayeux Tapestry Museum.

LINES FROM THE UNDERGROUND

On the way home,
in the tube,
I watched a girl
with a book of poems.

Her finger was flitting
back and forth,
like dialling a number
she wasn't sure of,
as though her eyes
were trying to find
one that could hold her
for a while.

Take her away,
set her on fire…

But aren't we all?

ET TU LEONARDO?

A little girl came in from the garden:
"Are you the man with poems in his head?"

"I… … might be!"

Dylan Thomas said,

"I have one in mine!" she replied,
"I eat the wind, I drink the rain…"

And Thomas thought: "Why should I then carry on?"
Or that, at least, was the implication.

And Betjeman, in a twilight quote said:
"When I think of what I knew I could have done
And what I did! You know, I wonder I went on…"

And da Vinci, on a failed fresco – he'd used braziers
To dry the paint and all his toil had melted
And rolled back down the wall, wrote:

"Always it seemed it was my fate
To work as though my efforts were but
sand upon a shore … …!"

So there we have it! The hopeless hovers,
Despite the silver lining, the busy flowers
Beneath the snow… …

For Betjeman, for Thomas (Dylan)
for Everyone!

Et Tu… … … …Leonardo?

PATHS TO THE SUN

                                                Met a
Couple on the plane, the woman said:
"I'd love to write a poem about clouds."

"Why don't you then?" I replied, "But
Maybe not that kind!" As I showed her
A wall of even grey, outside the plane's window.
"No, not that kind" her husband added,
"She means the sort you can fall into..."

Like arms or feathers or clear blue water.
Clouds you can munch.
Bite off and chew.
Clouds you could use as stepping stones
To where arrows land, shot from rainbows…

Clouds you could push in your pipe and smoke.
Clouds you tear off and wipe your nose.
Clouds you could throw around your shoulders
Or pull up under your chin…

Clouds, after a plunge in the sea, you could dry on,
Then on the beach, stretch out and get brown on.

Clouds you could gauge the speed of the wind by,
Then hail like a cab, for the ride of your life.

Clouds that would make stunning, wonderful photos
Or be used as background for Michelangelos'.

Clouds you could clamber and climb and read maps on,
When trying to find a path to the Sun.

CHAPTER 7

COMEDY SPOT

MAKE A LIST, LEST YE BE LOST

I've lost my list of "Things to do,"
I'm lost without my list!
Well, if not exactly "lost," let's face it:
Lacklustre... forlorn... limp
And... ... listless.

BEDSIDE COMPANIONS

My pin-up
       in black and white
with plait, bare breast
       and curving shoulder,
clipped at random
       from what must have been
a fairly decent newspaper.

Hope she doesn't mind
       being squeezed
between Kafka (Diaries)
       and King Lear.

JEALOUSY

It was the Poppers that did it!
She tore the place apart.
Having split, moved out,
Come back to the house to pick something up,
It was the poppers on the quilt cover
Went for the jugular, drove a skewer
Through her heart.

She happened to go up into the bedroom and
Noticed how for his new woman,
Everything was spicanspan…
For the first time! He'd bothered to hoover
And on the bedside table a vase
Of freshly bought flowers.

But all the roses of the East,
Lilies from the Song of Solomon,
Endless fields of Monet poppies,
Whole mountainsides of gentian.
All these would not have spurred the woman
To break the windows, smash the mirrors,
Tear the curtains from their rails
And in the ensuite bathroom,
Kick the basin from the wall.

A few fell swoops destroyed the room,
She saw green, she saw CRIMSON!
It was partly the flowers and partly the hoover
But mainly the fact that for Her, the BASTARD
Had taken the trouble (on the quilt cover)
                    To do up
    Every
              Single
                        Popper.

DON BE 100

[Number-plate seen on the autobahn, somewhere between Kassel and Hannover]

'WONDER & BE GLAD"

Don be a hundred, that's a reason
To wonder ...and be glad.
Don be a hundred an' 'e's
Fit as fiddle
And 'e does "you–know–what"
With the Missis still...
She told me that though,
It weren't 'im braggin'...
Don be a hundred, tha's
A reason to be glad!

'E can drink a pint, like me or you,
If the truth be known, 'e can drink a few
and find 'is own way 'ome alone,
If need be, under the Moon.
Don be a hundred, tha' should 'elp
to sweep away Old Sadness... 'e be
a hundred today, so let us all
Wonder and be glad.

ONLY JOKING

I'll really have to change this car,
THE BULB WENT! in the glove compartment,
Thus, "in the dark."
I ate some Blu Tack
mistaking it for Kendal Mint Cake.*

Legendary and required sustenance for mountaineers. Included in the official provisions for expeditions from Annapurna to Everest. A high-energy bar—sweet, green and minty—originally created for climbers in England's Lake District, and which my mother always gave me to take on my journeys.

NEW LIFE RESOLUTION!

I seem to have lost my Upateight
These days I sleep till Fartoolate
I need a boost of enthusiasm
To boldly, carefree, leap the chasm.
Without ado, I'll always then
Get up bright and early at seven.

JAK 359W

THE END OF A NEARER (and dearer)

Though only a car...

    CORTINA 1980 "W" 2 litre—Long Tax—MOT 9 months. "No Lady"
    owner but LONG DISTANCE RUNNER—Blaupunkt—£250 or nearest offer.

Many called but none came, until, after ten one night,
A guy in Clapham asked if I could bring it over. On the phone
He said: "Would you take a bit less?" and… "The main thing is:

        Will my family fit in?
        I have seven children!"

"How old are they?" I asked, imagining a sardine tin packed with
Footballers, disco ravers, long-gangly legs, pierced noses,
Reversed base-ball caps and smelly trainers…

"Well," he said, "they start at nine…"

"My God" I thought, "I'm right… it is, as described above!
Though… do they go up or down from nine?"

He hastened to add: "The youngest is three months."

So we drove the car over, his wife having asked on the phone:
"What colour ?" and he'd asked her: "'ow much cash have you got Love?"
And to me: "Would a hundred and ninety suffice?"

And when we got to the council estate and sounded the Cortina's horn,
He came down in a trice, the cash already in his hand, then his wife appeared
And said with a smile: "It looks aw' right!" And stood there, arms folded,
Quite excited.

So we went to the flat to exchange papers and, for them, my thrown-in
workshop manual.

The place was utterly filled with clutter and asleep on the sofa, there was an angel, about four, a long-blonde girl, a delicate and breathing treasure. And also a baba like a mini-Buddha, serene in sleep, miles away on a bouncy cot in the middle of the floor... and another character in this drama was Stallone (Sylvester) silent on the turned-down TV screen... and the one in the cot was of course The (real) Queen and we all had to talk in half-whispers, so as not to disturb her majesty.

They'd bought the car before they saw it, apologised for only having 190... so JAK, mi' ol' mate, here's one last job... ONE LAST JOURNEY:

My "long distance runner"—Oak tree seeker—Alone with the frost, Standing Stone companion—Autobahn pacer—My "By a lake stretch out and sleeper..." Courier to meet the Messenger of the Dawn...

Should you accept, this is your last assignment:

Do your best for them—Take 'em around—Show 'em a good time.

OCCUPATION:

HOUSE INSURANCE FORM—PUTNEY AREA—LONDON
[Liable to prosecution if you knowingly omit any relevant information]

I'm

A writer
    A facilitator,
        A poet,
            A decorator

A singer,
    An actor
        A luthier
            A carpenter

A musician
    A magician!
        A weaver
            A storyteller

A thinker
    A standandstare
        A troubadour
            A dreamer

"So, how are we doing? That's... among other things"

"Just a minute. Hang on, What does your main income stem from?"

"A race between: Decorator and Alltheothers put-together... in fact,
On second thoughts: The Latter... plus: a fair bit from some I forgot:

A listener to the wind
    A theatre director
        A hermit,
            A clown

A chewer of pencils
           A scribbler
                      A painter
                                  A jester,

A hanger of curtains
           A window cleaner
                      A washer up
                                A potato peeler

An entertainer
           A walker alone
                    A tree surgeon
                                A long distance driver

A visitor
           Of Old Peoples Homes
                    with a fistful of poems
                            and a ukulele…

"That's enough, that's enough… now you're getting silly!"

I'm a learner
           A teacher
                    A nothing-much-really

and as for the rest, I forget entirely. So, what do you think? Can you insure me?

"Certainly Sir. That'll be

                    A

                                  Million and one… Guineas!"*

For those too young to know, a guinea is "£1 and one shilling (5 pence)." An old-fashioned scheme for either "gilding" or "twisting the knife" while making a deal.

JUMPERS

What they call "Rag Rugs" are cheap.
You can get them at IKEA.
They're rough and ready but OK to lie on
And they come in nice, tasteful colours.

But then I noticed that here and there,
There were bits poking out, like butterflies sleeping,
"Oh shiii…!" I thought "No wonder they're cheap!"
But then, I suppose, if it came to that,
One could get a massage or even make love
On a field of unbreakable cotton wings,
Which'll be worn out within a year… but a
Friend from Cornwall said "Don't worry Brother!
You just pull 'em through from the other side,
That's what you do with jumpers."

I was amazed. Fancy that! Well I never!
He really knows about these things!
The world of cheap and cosy rugs
Has its own jargon.
There's a name for the wayward leaves of cotton,
They're called "Jumpers," Nice one!
But he hastened to add, he didn't mean that at all,
He was talking about sweaters, cardigans, you know,
Articles of clothing made from wool,
But from now on, for me, the first meaning of jumper
Will always remain
The bits of rag that rise from a rug and, as it were,
Have almost escaped.

So, in one's London terrace
Or leafy suburban street,
Remote and lonely cottage
Or tower-block council flat,
When by the gas or open fire,
"WATCH OUT!" There may be Jumpers there:
Before your very eyes
Salmon leaping through a roaring weir
Or Gazelles, legs rigid, almost flying
Across the rolling plains
Of Africa...

CHAPTER 8

THIS DARK WORLD AND WIDE

*"When I consider how my light is spent,
'Ere half my days in this dark world and wide..."*
John Milton

SHORT FRUITY POEM

"Cézanne has only to lay in one dab of colour,
it is nothing and it is beautiful."
Auguste Renoir

Sensuous poem
that aspires to be,
half as real
as Cézanne's apples:

Still Life, burning,
Frozen,
nothing more than
ripe fruit
lying on a table.

But LOOK intently,
for half a minute,
(Give the colours
time to bite)
And LISTEN
to them sing.

TASTE the flesh,
Let the juice run,

Breathe in
and SMELL the Seasons.

GET IN TOUCH,
through the knowledge of fruit,
with the essence
of all things.

THE ROSE THIEF

I am a Rose Thief, unashamed.
First I used up all of mine,
Then I scoured the well–heeled streets
(No need to break in, trample, trespass,
Tip–toe through the tight–lipped gardens);
In this area roses kindly
Burst out, spill over, boldly,
Brazenly let it be known:
"We have roses to spare."

So when, as I say, mine were all gone,
Cycle–mounted, I'd cruise the streets
And choose from cream, butter, vermilion
And then, I tested them for scent,
Without the pleasure this sense brings,
All that glorious choice of colour
Wouldn't mean a thing.

When I'd chosen two or three,
I took them...
Had I been frowned on, questioned, threatened,
I had prepared a case to take
To that Highest Court in the Land:

"These roses are going (Your 'Onour) I submit,
To Isobel,
Who clasps them like a crucifix,
Crushes them against her nose,
Closes her eyes and from them drinks
All ye need to know of Life
And every memory of joy,
For her, from almost a century.
Alone with me in this darkened room
In what we call an "Old People's"
But hardly is a home."

ICON

Girl on the pavement

With beret and bike;

Standing still as though

Holding a bridle. I've

Often wondered what it is

About women in berets? And she

Without trying, solved the riddle…

Now finally, I know.

It's a secular,

Stylish,

Soft spoken,

Representation

Of a halo.

NAMES OF TREES

> I'm amazed how many people don't know
> The names of trees and how indeed
> I don't myself, apart from the obvious,
> [Though only to me!]

The Birch for its sheddable, wedding-dress bark.
The Cedar for its dancers' outstretched hands.
The Rowan for its fists of orange berries.
The Oak for its leaves and its majesty.

The Pine for its needles and never-say-die
and almost pink of its sunburnt trunk.
The Cypress for its paint-brush directed at heaven,
Pulled to a point with finger and thumb.
The Willow for its whisper and the tales it tells
in stately homes on the banks of rivers.
The Holly for its joy and darkest of green,
Its standing alone and its tin-tack thorn.

But the Elm and Ash, the Larch and the Alder,
The Eucalyptus, the Deodar!
And the even more strange and extraordinary:
The Rosewood, which Germans call Palisander,
Palo Santo in Spanish (also Brazil),
Which means "Holy Wood," maybe we should
ALL go back to school

> Or wander through river gorge and canyon,
> Lonely moor, deep forest and field,
> With someone who knows the names of things
> Outside the cities of the world.

ANYTHING THAT'S GOING!

In the Old People's Home, I walked through what I call the "Salon,"
a long, tall drawing room—all the old faces, in armchairs facing
in no particular direction—Some of whom register surprise,
"Good cheer" even, when a stranger passes or comes in...
As I did and was waylaid: "Who are you? What's your name??"
"I'm Tony."
"Oh really, I don't think we've met!" ...then—eye to eye &
from the hip, the same vociferous lady added:
"Do you know Keith? He was here this morning but we missed each
other... if you see him, please tell him I'm waiting—He's a lovely young
man..."

When I came back an hour later, she grabbed me by the lapel again:
"Did you have any luck?" (with tracking down Keith – she awaited an
answer with bated breath).

Perhaps she imagined I'd been "all over:" To the Far East via Tangier,
asking questions in waterfront bars—
arm–wrestling in Samarkand with descendants of Genghis Khan—
masquerading with false passport —escaping from snow-bound
express trains—asking bandits and hermits and pale princesses living in
exile in mountain caves:
"I'm looking for a man named Keith?"
But always the same shake of the head: "I'm sorry but
please... ...share our meal and do, sleep through the Moon with us
if you like, before you rejoin the road."

Then finally, after months of wandering, I came across, on the
Cornish Coast, an Inn resembling The Admiral Benbow—crooked
ceilings, splintered timber, huge ingle–nook open fire and the company,
smoking curved clay pipes, fell silent when I mentioned Keith—the only
sound was the crackling logs and the inn-sign creaking on rusty iron. I
repeated: "Anyone seen him? Surely someone must know?? And a grey-
bearded voice from the corner said:
"Yes, 'e was 'ere... but that were *fifty* year ago.
I were barely in my teens and Demelza the barmaid there...
'Er mother wasn't even born..."

Chapter 8 - This Dark World and Wide

Well... I couldn't tell the lady this, when I got back to give my
report, so I simply said: "I'll keep my eyes skinned & if I may—
I'll carry on being your look–out."

Meanwhile, tea was being served... or coffee or Horlicks plus
biscuits and things. So I said, "Anyone fancy a song?" And took out the
ukulele. No-one answered, so not wishing to "barge in" or "come on too
strong," I said quietly to the "Keith lady:" "Would you like to hear a song?"
She replied, having left the question hanging:

"I'll take anything that's going!"

So I did "The Lamp–post"* by Mr. Formby, which lit a fire in
people's eyes...
"Oh me... Oh my:...
She'd never leave me flat,
She's not a girl like that!"

There's nothing like a good song...
For getting things going as, would you *believe?*
At that moment, out of the blue, KEITH arrived!
With a huge smile, said "Hello everyone,
frightfully sorry I'm late..." He was wearing
an RAF uniform, he'd just flown in,
having driven like hell
in the old MG to be there —

now that the War

was well...

and truly

over.

*The Lamp-post — refers to the song "Leaning on a Lamp Post" written by Noel Gay
(real name: Reginald Moxon Armitage) in 1937 and perhaps the best known song sung by
ukulele man George Formby.*

SEVEN YEARS TO DRAW A SWAN

On this space-suspended spinning stone,
We humans call The Earth,
With oceans and deserts and seething cities
And wild places of such beauty,
A poet would be stuck for words...
And men and women, after all these years,
Still fighting
For land, for gold, "what they believe," who
Just can't seem to find a way
To live in joy and peace...

Anyway..!

In this strange and jumbled place,
There once lived an Emperor of immense power,
On the other side of the World (from us),
Beyond Europe, beyond vast Russia,
I think it may have been Japan,
Or possibly even China...?

And deep in the folds of his far-flung lands,
Or so the story goes,
There was workin' away (so everyone said)
A truly wonderful Painter.

One lived in a palace as big as a town,
With bed-rooms the size of village halls,
And the other lived in a house on a hill
Which was not so big but then not small.
(And that will be IMPORTANT as this story unfolds)
With a view of a valley and winding river
And trees which, in the wind,
Tossed their heads, shrugged their shoulders
And stretched their arms like dancers.

The Emperor summoned the Painter and said
"Draw me a swan, for this I will pay
A hundred glistening, gleaming jewels,"
And the Painter said "Your Majesty,

Gladly I'll perform your command...,
If you will kindly make it a thousand."

Thinking (strictly to himself);
"I'll keep a couple as my own,
Then give one to every village
And a handful to every town
And take the long way home."

The Emperor didn't hear his thoughts
But didn't like what he said one bit,
Replied: "I (whatever his name was...)
The emperor...
How dare you bargain...?"
But he managed to keep his anger tucked
And rolled beneath his chin,
All because of his deep–down need,
For this drawing of a swan.
And anyway, what were jewels to him?
He had cellars full... millions of the things....
Perhaps that was why he really wanted
A unique and eternal painting.

"Bring him the best, the finest parchment,
Silk to paint on, anything he wants.
Brushes of the softest fur, sable, squirrel, spare no expense."

Then the painter interrupted: "With respect,
Your... er ...Royal Highness,
I must now go back to my house on the hill.
Out of the question for me to work here,
And anyway... didn't I say?
The task will take me seven years."

So off he went to his house on the hill
(which was not so big but then not small)
A different way from that he had come
And gave a jewel to every village
And a handful to every town
And took the long way home.

Seven years pass of sun and snow,
Harvest, weddings, deaths, we all know,
How the seasons freeze and burn
And how Time... so quickly goes.

Then with elephants and clowns and soldiers,
(Everything an Emperor thinks he needs),
The journey began to the end of his Lands,
He thought:
"Now I shall have my Swan!"

And when it came to the house on the hill,
(Not so big but then... not small)
His caravan shuddered still,
The weary soldiers mopping their sweat
And the elephants thinking: "Thank God for that!"

The Painter was waiting and ushered them in,
The Emperor said: "I see no swan!"
And sure enough, in the bare room,
All there was, was a large canvas
With not a brush-stroke on, so

Everyone was speechless with surprise
As the painter selected his finest sable,
Put his working tunic on
And began to paint before their eyes
What would soon become a swan.

The emperor's face went from red to purple
And then to a ghastly white.
"How dare you?! you have mocked me" he said,
"A thousand jewels and seven years
And only then you begin to paint my swan
As if, in this world, you hadn't a care!"

But nobody heard The Emperor's words,
Something very strange was happening:
Taking shape on the canvas was
the most extraordinary thing —
As the brush twisted, hissed and bent

It seemed they'd been taken out of Time
Or just arrived in some unknown land
And a spell... had fallen on them...
No-one could believe their eyes,
A swan which, till then, was never seen.
A swan in a way beyond all swans
Of unbelievable beauty.

And the painter might well have been quite alone,
So deep he was in concentration.
And in precisely seven minutes,
The painting was signed and done.

"SEIZE HIM!" screamed the Emperor,
By now, beside himself with anger,

"First he must die a thousand deaths
And then his head will roll..."

It was one of those moments,
(you may know what I mean),
When the whole world seems out of tune,

The clocks go round the other way,
Fish grow feathers and fly from the sea,
The Moon shines warm and the Sun turns pale
Rain coils upwards and smoke falls.

They carried the painter out in chains,
With ropes and daggers and manacles,
But the emperor's son, an intelligent one,
As princes go, remained there in the room,
When all the others had gone,
Held by the spirit of the swan
And by the feeling that something
Was absolutely and terribly wrong...

He began to wander through the house on the hill
(which was not so big but then... not small)
And now you will see why
I had to mention this at all, for

As he went from room to room
Still in a daze and on his own,
There on every single wall,
On easels, canvasses, even the floor!
Everywhere imaginable...:
He saw thousands of swans in scores of styles.

On the windows, scribbled on curtains,
A myriad images of swans:
Abstract, flying, just a few lines.
In immense and every-feather detail.
Swans with necks like curling snakes,
Poised and reared, about to strike,
Or just a shadow beneath the surface,
A white sword in a dark lake.
Swans from every way of life,
On palace pool and village pond,
Angry swans, swans of the mind,
And swans with necks stiff as arrows
Cutting across or through the wind.

And thus the prince's heavy load,
Fell like a sack, slashed from his shoulders,
He ran to the Emperor and said: "Father, come
And I think you will let this Painter go."

Seven years of concentration.
Seven thousand (or more!) swans
Practising and Learning to draw The One,
Barely thinking and hardly trying.

So The Emperor set the Painter free
And headed home clutching his treasure
And when his caravan was simply
Dust on the horizon,
The Painter walked down to the river,
Stayed all night until the dawn,
Listened to the voices of the Wind,
And watched the clouds, some quite like swans,
Gliding past the Moon.

FROM THE TRACK THROUGH THE PINES TO THE COPPER SEA

When I was a lad, must have been about ten,
I heard a song called "The Erlkoenig."
It was on the radio and sung in German
And it made me shiver all the way to my bones!

I'd rather *not* tell you the story,
As it was then (and still is) far too scary!
So I'll give you hints of it, that'll be best,
Let the Piano and the Singer's Voice do the rest.

The Pianist's hands up and down the keys
Are the wind in the forest or wild beasts,
They are shadows that move and have a life of their own.
They're the mist like ghosts moving through the pines

And the horses hooves drumming, galloping on,
Icicles breaking and freezing rain...
All this from ten fingers making felt hammers ring
And a man's voice which manages to sing

For *three* people: A Father, his Son and The Elfin King.
Changing register to suit each one,
In a spell-binding, three–way conversation:

"Father, help me! The Elf King is calling!"

"Hush my son, it's only the wind!"

Then the King says "Come, my daughters are waiting
By crystal fountains, fine games to begin."

As I've said, when I was a lad,
I realized what could be done—
How music can send shivers–down–the–spine!!
And *another* piece that really inspired
Was the overture to Scheherazade,

Which, in a way, is the story of stories
And comes from Arabia where the sky
Is the brightest possible shiny blue,
Where the women wear trousers of shimmering silk
And the men: Turbans and curly shoes…

For those of you that don't know what happened,
The tale begins with a "wicked" Sultan
Who, because his wife had been unfaithful
Had her strangled without a trial;
Married again every night from then on,
Putting the new wife to death at dawn.

Scheherazade, a beautiful girl,
Who'd also done very well at school,
Thought *"This is ridiculous… …I can <u>right</u> this wrong!"*
So she got herself selected as wife
And, as part of a careful and subtle plan,
Asked if she could take her sister along.
A couple of hours before the dawn,
[the time when the axe, so to speak, was to fall]
The sister said sweetly to Scheherazade:
"Please, will you tell me *one last story!*"

The Sultan agreed and said: "Don't make it too long!"
To which Scheherazade replied: "My Lord,
I'll make it no longer than you can stand.
No stronger nor fragile than the wind.
No brighter nor terrifying than water,
And My Lord, you would do well to remember
That drops of rain when bound together,
Will form a chain and make a river
Which may become a lake and then
Eventually an ocean!" With this,
To her sister, she began:

"Long, long ago there lived a merchant…"

All ears, her sister, Dinazarde,
Placed her chin in the cup of her hands

And the Sultan too was secretly listening
Exactly as Scheherazade had planned!
So that, when the time came for her execution,
The Sultan said, "But I must know how the story ends!
I simply HAVE to hear the rest!"
Scheherazade shrugged her lovely shoulders
And said, "My Lord, I don't know WHAT to suggest?!"

"CANCEL THE EXECUTION!" he said (or at least "postpone")
"One more night you will stay with me but you die tomorrow at dawn!"

But "one more night" became another and another
As the stories followed each other on
And just as Scheherazade had said,
They joined together like drops of rain
And indeed became an ocean, for nights in number 1001
When, by then they had three children!

And the Executioner, out of a job,
Took up fishing instead —
Spent his dawns and days by the river
Was happier and kinder and slept better in bed.

And the music for this is by Rimsky-Korsakov.
When I was a kid, I thought his *christian* name was Rimsky,
(you know): Son of Mr. and Mrs. Korsakov
Though my better informed friends said
"That's not his *christian* name,
Rimsky! Ofcourseit'snot!!"

But until I knew better, I imagined Rimsky's Russian mother
Shouting: "Rimsky come in, it's time for supper
Or "Rimsky come in and practice your piano
    How many times must I tell you!?"

In fact, his name was Nicolas and he was nowhere to be found.
He was out in the woods, on the ridge, by the lake,
Watching the sun go down…
And dreaming of faraway lands and
Ships setting sail on copper seas,

Hearing already in his head, tunes
On the wood–wind and violin…
Percussion in the spiders' webs
And timpani in the trees.

And I think it's relevant to tell you,
I wrote a song when my Mum passed on,
Which went *and still goes!*

"My Mama loved the violin,
People like Mozart and Mendelsohn
And the fiddle that winds its way like a road
Or river through Scheherazade…"

RADIO

Luxembourg* transmitted magic
On a shoestring—on a broomstick.
Sought out the windy boarding–school,
Got lost, came back, crackled, whistled—
Brought us Holly the Magician,
His new single "Rave On," which cuts a piano into stars,
And dances then on broken glass…
This I heard under blankets
For the first time, in the dead of night;

Just like "Le Mans," the bulletin at one; all good
Children fast asleep—but me transported to Gallic poplars,
Willing on the shark-sleek, dark-green D–type Jaguar.

Talking of cars, years ago,
Radios were seldom standard.
I fitted mine to the Anglia Van.
It took almost a whole week–end.
I cast the net again and again
But not a sound till, out of the blue:
A woman's voice! I'll never know – What did I do?
A voice singing to six strings only,
The song called "Willie o' Winsbury," which ends:
"The lovers were given as much land
As they could ride in a Summer's day."
Had the radio packed up there and then,
I had my money's worth… times ten.

This miracle, in a dream, I offered to my friend Aladdin:
"Put it beside the Horse with Wings.
At the turn of a knob," I said "this casket
Will bring you All the World… can also
Speak to you… … … and sing."

Radio Luxembourg

POEM FOR MR BOYD – THE POET

In memory of

Clearing out his cupboard under the stairs,
We put the smallest: Young Fiona.
within the cramped and dingy space,

formed a chain, three generations long.
The child of the company, stationed,
as it were, within the chimney and
as she handed me all manner of things,
We formed another chain (or link)
back through the years...

as every object turned a page,
took us down forgotten corridors,
Flung open creaking windows
On another age.

I presented them to Mr. Boyd,
sitting in state, on a wooden chair,
as "Lord of the Manor!" he later suggested
or, as I said "Emperor!!"
endowed with the power of Life or Death:
"To Sanctuary on the garage shelf!"
and others, whose only sin
was "worn out..." "no further use,"
Consigned to the rubbish bin.

I unwrapped shapes in shrouds of shredded
yellow newspaper "What's in there?"
he'd say and fix me
with a quizzical stare,
"Judging by its weight, it must be metal
or possibly even LEAD!"
"That's a tool, from the soles of boots
for extracting steel studs,
and that chocolate–coloured bakelite thing,
with handle and strange–shaped holes,

That's a wool–cutter (you mightn't remember),
for use when making rugs,"
And sure enough, hot on its heels,
a grimy bundled–up net —
a tangled skeleton of thread,
its little squares blocked by dust
and ancient, obsolete cobwebs.

And thus unfolded before our eyes
evidence
              of recent History
only seen, for decades,
by spiders and scurrying mice:
A rusty, twisted fire–guard,
tins of dried–out "Cherry Blossom."*
their contents
              rattling like dice.

The job well done, the cupboard bare,
He made us a quality cup of tea,
with cream cake, by a flickering fire,
(Old Masters blu–tacked to the faded tiles)
and when we left, he gave me a book
of
        Modern Irish Poetry.

In the Mourne Mountains, where it resides,
May his Spirit flit with well–read Faeries,
discuss and tramp on green hillsides
and look out
              over the sea.

Name of a shoe polish colour in the UK.

ANSWERING DAD BACK

What have you achieved this week?
His gentle question stuck in my ear.
What have you achieved this week?
I hear it ringing down the years,
The thousand times the boy has racked his brains –
Let me see! Let me see!
What can I drum up, present for scrutiny?!
So, what have I achieved this week
Let me see! Let me see!
I earned a couple of hundred quid,
Painting an apartment,
Not sure that even registers
On the metre of achievement?
I had a chat in Sainsbury's
With a friendly cashier,
She told me 'bout her holiday,
"Mykonos" this year!
So, what have I achieved?
Let me see! Let me see!
Not very much, I'd say,
If this poem's to be believed
But there was one thing,
Maybe this, seriously.

In your house, at the beginning of the week,
This cold, dark January,
I got up at ten past six,
Drew the curtains, half asleep,
In the night the frost had come,
Jack Frost, the famous one,
And covered everything in sight
With sparkling jewellery:
The cricket field, the russet pine,
The iron railings, the washing line,
The bird table, the wooden fence,
The garage roof, the bare stems of creepers
And the sleeping flowers,
EVERYTHING!

Sizzling, bubbling in the cauldron
Of Winter's alchemy—
I stood and gazed for twenty minutes,
Through the steam from a cup of tea.

So what have I achieved?
No feat of great renown but
I've seen the visible world
on a winter's dawn
And managed...
to write it down.

GLOSSARY

This selected glossary of words, names and terms is added for the convenience of readers to enhance their enjoyment of, and access to, the full range of language and meaning used in the poems, particular for American readers. The briefest definition or explanation is provided only to support the meaning in the poem. Of course alternative definitions exist and these can be found in any good dictionary, thesaurus or encyclopedia. The glossary is presented in alphabetical order to avoid the need to repeat words that appear in more than one poem.

Anglia Van: Refers to the Ford Anglia. A British car designed and manufactured by Ford in the United Kingdom. It is related to the Ford Prefect and the later Ford Popular. The Ford Anglia name was applied to four models of car between 1939 and 1967. 1,594,486 Anglia's were produced, before it was replaced by the new Ford Escort. In the US this is known as a "panel truck."

Anne Sylvestre: Real name is Anne-Marie Beugras, born 20 June 1934 in Lyon, France, is a French singer-songwriter.

Bakelite: An early plastic. It was developed by Belgian-born chemist Leo Baekeland in New York in 1907. One of the first plastics made from synthetic components, Bakelite was used for its electrical nonconductivity and heat-resistant properties in electrical insulators, radio and telephone casings, and such diverse products as kitchenware, jewelry, pipe stems, and children's toys.

Brigid's crosses: Brighid's cross or Brigit's cross (Irish: Cros Bríde, Crosóg Bríde or Bogha Bríde) is an Irish symbol. Though a Christian symbol, it possibly derives from the pagan sunwheel. It is usually made from rushes or, less often, straw. It comprises a woven square in the centre and four radials tied at the ends. Brigid's crosses are associated with Brigid of Kildare, who is venerated as one of the patron saints of Ireland

Blake, William: (28 November 1757 – 12 August 1827) was an English poet, painter, and printmaker. Largely unrecognised during his lifetime, Blake is now considered a seminal figure in the history of the poetry and visual arts of the Romantic Age. His prophetic poetry has been said to form "what is in proportion to its merits the least read body of poetry in the English language." His visual artistry led one contemporary art critic to proclaim him "far and away the greatest artist Britain has ever produced."

Blu-Tack: A reusable putty-like pressure-sensitive adhesive produced by Bostik, commonly used to attach lightweight objects (such as posters or sheets of paper) to walls or other dry surfaces. Traditionally pale blue, it is also available in other colours.

Brylcream(ed): A brand of hair styling products for men sold worldwide. The first Brylcreem product was a pomade created in 1928 by County Chemicals at the Chemico Works in Bradford Street, Birmingham, England. The pomade is an emulsion of water and mineral oil stabilised with beeswax.

Cherry Blossom: Cherry Blossom, a UK manufacturer of boot polish, in various colours, has been in continuous production since 1903.

Coulee Dam: The Grand Coulee Dam is a gravity dam on the Columbia River in the U.S. State of Washington built to produce hydroelectric power and provide irrigation. It was constructed between 1933 and 1942, originally with two power plants. It is the largest electric power-producing facility in the United States and one of the largest concrete structures in the world. Commissioned to write a songs about the coming opening Woody Guthrie in 1941 wrote "Grand Coulee Dam." Tony heard this song from Lonnie Donegan who recorded it in the UK.

Demelza: A girl's name of Cornish origin, and the meaning of Demelza is "fort on the hill." First used as a given name in the 1950s.

Deodar: Cedrus deodara, is a species of cedar native to the western Himalayas in eastern Afghanistan, northern Pakistan, northern India, occurring at 1,500–3,200 m (4,921–10,499 ft) altitude. It is a large evergreen coniferous tree and has a conic crown with level branches and drooping branches.

Descant Recorders: A musical wind instrument made of wood, with a range of 2 octaves starting from C above middle C and very thin. Descant means Soprano.

Dylan Marlais Thomas: (27 October 1914 – 9 November 1953) was a Welsh poet and writer whose works include the poems "Do not go gentle into that good night" and "And death shall have no dominion," the "play for voices," Under Milk Wood, and stories and radio broadcasts such as *A Child's Christmas in Wales* and *Portrait of the Artist as a Young Dog*. He became popular in his lifetime, and remained so after his death, partly because of his larger than life character and his reputation for drinking to excess. Thomas was born in Swansea, Wales in 1914. An undistinguished student, he left school at 16, becoming a journalist for a short time. Although many of his works appeared in print while he was still a teenager, it was the publication of "Light breaks where no sun shines," in 1934, that caught the attention of the literary world. While living in London, Thomas met Caitlin Macnamara, whom he married in 1937, eventually settling in the Welsh fishing village of Laugharne.

Ely Cathedral: (in full, The Cathedral Church of the Holy and Undivided Trinity of Ely) is the principal church of the Diocese of Ely, in Cambridgeshire, England, and is the seat of the Bishop of Ely and a suffragan bishop, the Bishop of Huntingdon. It is known locally as "the ship of the Fens," because of its prominent shape that towers above the surrounding flat and watery landscape. Most of what is known about the early history of Ely comes from Bede's *Historia ecclesiastica gentis Anglorum* and above all from the *Liber Eliensis*, an anonymous chronicle written at Ely some time in the 12th century and covering the history of the Abbey and Cathedral from 673 until the mid-12th century.

Equus: A genus of animals in the family Equidae that includes horses, donkeys, and zebras.

Everly Brothers: (Isaac Donald "Don" Everly, born February 1, 1937, and Phillip "Phil" Everly, born January 19, 1939) were American country-influenced rock and roll singers, known for steel-string guitar playing and close harmony singing. The duo was elected to the Rock and Roll Hall of Fame in 1986.

Feste: A fictional character—the clown, fool or court jester—in the William Shakespeare's comedy *Twelfth Night*. He is attached to the household of the Countess Olivia.

Fleur-de-lys (plural: fleurs-de-lis): A stylized lily (in French, fleur means flower, and lis means lily) or iris that is used as a decorative design or symbol. It may be "at one and the same time, religious, political, dynastic, artistic, emblematic, and symbolic," especially in French heraldry. While the fleur-de-lis has appeared on countless European coats of arms and flags over the centuries, it is particularly associated with the French monarchy in an historical context, and continues to appear in the arms of the King of Spain and the Grand Duke of Luxembourg and members of the House of Bourbon. It remains an enduring symbol of France that appears on French postage stamps, although it has never been adopted officially by any of the French republics.

Ford Cortina: A family car built by Ford of Britain in various guises from 1962 to 1982. The Cortina was Ford's mass-market compact car and became Britain's best-selling car of the 1970s. The Cortina was produced in five generations (Mark I through to Mark V, although officially the last one was called the Cortina 80) from 1962 until 1982.

Formby, George: (26 May 1904 – 6 March 1961), A British comedy actor, singer-songwriter and comedian. He sang light, comical songs, usually playing the ukelele. He was a major star of stage and screen in the 1930s and 1940s.

Gallic poplars: Reference to the French tree that grows around the route of the Le Mans race track in France.

Georges Brassens: (French: 22 October 1921 – 29 October 1981), was a French singer-songwriter and poet. Brassens was born in Sète, a town in southern France near Montpellier. Now an iconic figure in France, he achieved fame through his elegant songs with their harmonically complex music for voice and guitar and articulate, diverse lyrics; indeed, he is considered one of France's most accomplished postwar poets.

George Herbert: (3 April 1593 – 1 March 1633) was a Welsh-born English poet, orator and Anglican priest. Herbert's poetry is associated with the writings of the metaphysical poets, and he is recognized as "a pivotal figure: enormously popular, deeply and broadly influential, and arguably the most skillful and important British devotional lyricist."

Green Men: [Green man] is a sculpture, drawing, or other representation of a face surrounded by or made from leaves. Branches or vines may sprout from the nose, mouth, nostrils or other parts of the face and these shoots may bear flowers or fruit. Commonly used as a decorative architectural ornament, Green Men are frequently found on carvings in churches and other buildings (both secular and ecclesiastical). The Green Man motif has many variations. Found in many cultures from many ages around the world, the Green Man is often related to natural vegetative deities. It is primarily interpreted as a symbol of rebirth, representing the cycle of growth each spring. Some speculate that the mythology of the Green Man developed independently in the traditions of separate ancient cultures and evolved into the wide variety of examples found throughout history.

Griffin: The griffin, griffon, or gryphon is a legendary creature with the body, tail, and back legs of a lion; the head and wings of an eagle; and an eagle's talons as its front feet. While griffins are most common in the art and lore of Ancient Greece, there is evidence of representations of griffins in Ancient Persian and Ancient Egyptian art as far back as 3,300 BC.

Heine, Heinrich: (13 December 1797 – 17 February 1856) born Harry Heine, changed to Christian Johann Heinrich Heine following his conversion to Christianity from Judaism. One of the most significant German poets of the 19th century. He was also a journalist, essayist, and literary critic. He is best known outside Germany for his early lyric poetry, which was set to music in the form of Lieder (art songs) by composers such as Robert Schumann and Franz Schubert. Heine's later verse and prose is distinguished by its satirical wit and irony. His radical political views led to many of his works being banned by German authorities. Heine spent the last 25 years of his life as an expatriate in Paris.

Hoban, Russell Conwell: (February 4, 1925 – December 13, 2011) born in Lansdale, Pennsylvania, was an American writer. His works span many genres, including fantasy, science fiction, mainstream fiction, magical realism, poetry, and children's books. He lived in London, England, from 1969 until his death.

Hokey Cokey: Called, hokey pokey (United States, Canada, Ireland, Australia), hokey tokey (New Zealand), also known as okey cokey, or cokey cokey, is a dance with a distinctive accompanying tune and lyric structure. It is well known in English-speaking countries.

Icarus: In Greek mythology, Icarus is the son of the master craftsman Daedalus. The main story told about Icarus is his attempt to escape from Crete by means of wings that his father constructed from feathers and wax. He ignored instructions not to fly too close to the sun, and the melting wax caused him to fall into the sea where he drowned.

Jacques Brel: (8 April 1929 – 9 October 1978) was a Belgian singer-songwriter who composed and performed literate, thoughtful, and theatrical songs that generated a large, devoted following in Belgium and France initially, and later throughout the world.

John Betjeman, (Sir): (28 August 1906 – 19 May 1984) was an English poet, writer and broadcaster. Starting his career as a journalist, he ended it as one of the most popular British Poets Laureate and a much-loved figure on British television. He was a founding member of the Victorian Society and a passionate defender of Victorian architecture.

John Donne: (between 24 January and 19 June 1572 – 31 March 1631) An English poet, satirist, lawyer and a cleric in the Church of England. He is considered the pre-eminent representative of the metaphysical poets. His works are noted for their strong, sensual style and include sonnets, love poetry, religious poems, Latin translations, epigrams, elegies, songs, satires and sermons. His poetry is noted for its vibrancy of language and inventiveness of metaphor, especially compared to that of his contemporaries.

John Keats: (31 October 1795 – 23 February 1821) An English Romantic poet. He was one of the main figures of the second generation of Romantic poets along with Lord Byron and Percy Bysshe Shelley. Although his poems were not generally well received by critics during his life, his reputation grew after his death, so that by the end of the 19th century he had become one of the most beloved of all English poets.

Julius Caesar, Gaius: (3 July 100 BC – 15 March 44 BC) A Shakespearian tragedy. He was a Roman general, statesman, Consul and notable author of Latin prose. He played a critical role in the events that led to the demise of the Roman Republic and the rise of the Roman Empire. In 60 BC, Caesar, Crassus and Pompey formed a political alliance that was to dominate Roman politics for several years. Their attempts to amass power through populist tactics were opposed by the conservative elite within the Roman Senate, among them Cato the Younger with the frequent support of Cicero. Caesar's conquest of Gaul, completed by 51 BC, extended Rome's territory to the English Channel and the Rhine. Caesar became the first Roman general to cross both when he built a bridge across the Rhine and conducted the first invasion of Britain.

Jumper: Similar to a sweater in the US, which is pulled on over the head, in the UK, Ireland, and Commonwealth.

Kendal Mint Cake: This is a glucose-based confection flavoured with peppermint. It originates from Kendal in Cumbria, England. Kendal Mint Cake is popular among climbers and mountaineers, especially those from the United Kingdom, as a source of energy.

King James: Refers to King James II of England & VII of Scotland defeated by King William III.

King Stone: [see The Rollright Stones].

King William: From 1689 he reigned as William III over England and Ireland; it is a coincidence that his regnal number (III) was the same for both Orange and England. He is informally known by sections of the population in Northern Ireland [created in 2921] and Scotland as "King Billy." In what became known as the "Glorious Revolution," on 5 November 1688 William invaded England in an action that ultimately deposed King James II & VII and won him the crowns of England, Scotland and Ireland. In the British Isles, William ruled jointly with his wife, Mary II. The period of their joint reign is often referred to as "William and Mary." A Protestant, William participated in several wars against the powerful Catholic king of France, Louis XIV, in coalition with Protestant and Catholic powers in Europe. Many Protestants heralded him as a champion of their faith. Largely because of that reputation, William was able to take the British crowns when many were fearful of a revival of Catholicism under James. William's victory over James at the Battle of the Boyne, Ireland, in 1690 is still commemorated by the Orange Order in Northern Ireland.

Kristoffer "Kris" Kristofferson: (born June 22, 1936) An American country music singer, songwriter, musician, and film actor.

La Chanson Poétique: French translation of Song Poetry or Art Song.

Mandala: Is a generic term for any plan, chart or geometric pattern that represents the cosmos metaphysically or symbolically; a microcosm of the universe from an enlightened perspective; i.e., that of the principal deity. It is a spiritual and ritual symbol in Hinduism and Buddhism, representing the Universe. The basic form of most mandalas is a square with four gates containing a circle with a center point. Each gate is in the general shape of a T. Mandalas often exhibit radial balance. The term is of Hindu origin.

Mark Antony: (Marcus Antonius, January 14, 83 BC – August 1, 30 BC), was a Roman politician and general. As a military commander and administrator, he was an important supporter and loyal friend of his mother's cousin Julius Caesar. After Caesar's assassination, Antony formed an official political alliance with Octavian (the future Augustus) and Lepidus, known to historians today as the Second Triumvirate.

Mick Linnard and David Hughes: British guitar duo of the late 70s 80s, with a number of fine albums and great friends of Tony Maude. See website: www.davidhughes.com for more details. In 2004 Mick moved to the US and in 2006, and with his wife Tamara Martin founded Little Red Tree Publishing (www.littleredtree.com) and is the publisher of this book, .

Monty Python: Monty Python (sometimes known as The Pythons) were a British surreal comedy group that created Monty Python's Flying Circus, a British television comedy sketch show that first aired on the BBC on 5 October 1969. Forty-five episodes were made over four series. The Python phenomenon developed from the television series into something larger in scope and impact, spawning touring stage shows, films, numerous albums, several books and a stage musical as well as launching the members to individual stardom. The group's influence on comedy has been compared to The Beatles' influence on music.

Mourne Mountains: Also called the Mournes or Mountains of Mourne, (Irish - na Beanna Bóirche) are a granite mountain range in County Down in the south-east of Northern Ireland. It includes the highest mountains in Northern Ireland and the province of Ulster. The Mournes is an area of outstanding natural beauty and has been proposed as the first national park in Northern Ireland. The name Mourne (historically spelt Morne) is derived from the name of a Gaelic clann or sept called the Múghdhorna.

Morton, Henry Canova Vollam (H. V.), FRSL: (26 July 1892–18 June 1979) was a journalist and pioneering travel writer from Lancashire, England, best known for his prolific and popular books on Britain and the Holy Land. He first achieved fame in 1923 when, while working for the Daily Express, he scooped the official Times correspondent during the coverage of the opening of the Tomb of Tutankhamon by Howard Carter in Egypt.

New College: One of the many Colleges that make up Oxford University. Despite its name, New College is one of the oldest of the Oxford colleges: it was founded in 1379 by William of Wykeham, Bishop of Winchester as "The College of St Mary of Winchester in Oxford", the second college in Oxford to be dedicated to the Blessed Virgin Mary.

Norman stone: This refers to the fact that after the Norman conquest of Great Britain, stone was use to build structures, mainly churches and Castles replacing wood used by the Anglo Saxons to that time. Of course there were many stone building abandoned by the Romans but by 1066 they were 600-700 years old and mostly in ruins. Spelsbury church was an example.

Ojibway: (also Ojibwa or Ojibwe, Anishinaabe, also Anishinabe or Chippewa, also Chippeway) are the largest groups of Native Americans–First Nations north of Mexico. They are divided between Canada and the United States. In the United States, they had the fourth-largest population among Native American tribes, surpassed only by Navajo, Cherokee and the Lakota. Because many Ojibway were historically formerly located mainly around the outlet of Lake Superior, which the French colonists called Sault Ste. Marie, they referred to the Ojibway as Saulteurs. The Ojibway peoples are a major component group of the Anishinaabe-speaking peoples, a branch of the Algonquian language family which includes the Algonquin, Nipissing, Oji-Cree, Odawa and the Potawatomi. The Ojibwe Nation was the first to set the agenda with European-Canadian leaders for signing more detailed treaties before many European settlers were allowed too far west.

Paul Millns: British musician and singer-songwriter of immense talent and great friend of Tony's, living in Putney, London. See website: www.paulmillns.com for more details.

Paul Simon: (born October 13, 1941) is an American musician and singer-songwriter. Simon's fame, influence, and commercial success began as part of the duo Simon & Garfunkel, formed in 1964 with musical partner Art Garfunkel. Simon wrote most of the pair's songs, including three that reached No. 1 on the U.S. singles charts: "The Sound of Silence", "Mrs. Robinson", and "Bridge Over Troubled Water".The duo split up in 1970 at the height of their popularity, and Simon began a successful solo career as a guitarist and singer-songwriter, recording three highly acclaimed albums over the next five years. In 1986, he released *Graceland*, an album inspired by South African township music.

Peter, Paul and Mary: They were a US folk-singing trio whose nearly 50-year career began with their rise to become a paradigm for 1960s folk music. The trio was composed of Peter Yarrow, (Noel) Paul Stookey and Mary Travers. After the death of Mary Travers in 2009, Yarrow and Stookey continued to perform as a duo under their individual names.

Poppers: Is a term used in the UK to describe snap fasteners.

Poulnabrone dolmen (Poll na mBrón in Irish, meaning "hole of the quern stones") is a portal tomb in County Clare, Ireland, dating back to the Neolithic period, probably between 4200 BCE and 2900 BCE.

Puccini, Giacomo Antonio Domenico Michele Secondo Maria: (22 December 1858 – 29 November 1924), generally known as Giacomo Puccini, was an Italian composer whose operas are among the most frequently performed in the standard repertoire. Puccini has been called "the greatest composer of Italian opera after Verdi."

Radio Luxembourg: Started in 1933 from the Grand Duchy of Luxembourg, and was the forerunner to the Pirate Radio Station, that broadcast from ships moored off the coast of southern England. In the 1960's it enabling a whole generation to listen to the latest hits on "crystal sets."

Regal Orange sword: Refers to the sword of King William III of

England and Prince of Orange of the House of Orange-Nassau [know as William of Orange], which was used in the battles against Protestant King Louis XIV of France, and James II of England. Frequently depicted in wall murals scattered all over Northern Ireland.

Riddley Walker: A science fiction novel by Russell Hoban, first published in 1980. It won the John W. Campbell Memorial Award for best science fiction novel in 1982, as well as an Australian Science Fiction Achievement Award in 1983. It was additionally nominated for the Nebula Award for Best Novel in 1981.

Rimsky-Korsakov, Nikolai Andreyevich: (18 March 1844–21 June 1908) was a Russian composer. He was a master of orchestration. His best-known orchestral compositions—*Capriccio Espagnol*, the *Russian Easter Festival Overture*, and the symphonic suite *Scheherazade*—along with suites and 15 operas. *Scheherazade* is an example of his frequent use of fairy tale and folk subjects.

River Wey: A river that runs throught the English counties of Surrey, Hampshire [many hop-fields found along its banks] and West Sussex and a tributary of the River Thames with two separate branches that join at Tilford. The name may be derived from the Old English word Éa meaning "river."

Rollright Stones: A complex of three Neolithic and Bronze Age megalithic monuments located near to the village of Long Compton on the borders of Oxfordshire and Warwickshire in the English Midlands. Constructed from local oolitic limestone, the three separate monuments, now known as The King's Men, The King Stone and The Whispering Knights, are each distinct in their design and purpose, and were each built at different periods in late prehistory. The stretch of time during which the three monuments were erected here bears witness to a continuous tradition of ritual behaviour on sacred ground, from the 4th to the 2nd millennium BCE.

Rudyard Kipling: (30 December 1865 – 18 January 1936) An English short-story writer, poet, and novelist chiefly remembered for his tales and poems of British soldiers in India and his tales for children. He was born in Bombay, in the Bombay Presidency of British India, and was taken by his family to England when he was five years old. Kipling is best known for his works of fiction, including *The Jungle Book* (a collection of stories which includes "Rikki-Tikki-Tavi"), *Just So Stories* (1902), *Kim* (1901), many short stories, including "The Man Who Would Be King" (1888); and his poems, including "Mandalay" (1890), "Gunga Din" (1890), "The White Man's Burden" (1899) and "If—" (1910). In 1907 he was awarded the Nobel Prize in Literature, making him the first English-language writer to receive the prize, and to date he remains its youngest recipient. Among other honours, he was sounded out for the British Poet Laureateship and on several occasions for a knighthood, all of which he declined.

R.U.C.: The Royal Ulster Constabulary (RUC) was the police force in Northern Ireland from 1922 to 2000. Following the awarding of the George Cross in 2000, it was subsequently known as the Royal Ulster Constabulary GC. It was founded on 1 June 1922 out of the Royal Irish Constabulary (RIC).

Samarkand: The second-largest city in Uzbekistan and the capital of Samarqand Province. The city is most noted for its central position on the Silk Road between China and the West, and for being an Islamic centre for scholarly study.

Scheherazade: Name of a legendary Persian queen and the storyteller of *One Thousand and One Nights*.

Siegfried and Brunhilde: Two characters from the Grand Opera of Richard Wagner's (1813–1883) "The Ring of the Nibelung." It is a cycle of four epic operas. The works are based loosely on characters from the Norse sagas and the Nibelungenlied. The operas, which the composer described as a trilogy with a Vorabend ("ante-evening"), are often referred to as the Ring cycle, Wagner's Ring, or simply the Ring. The operas are: Das Rheingold (The Rhine Gold), Die Walküre (The Valkyrie), Siegfried, and Götterdämmerung (Twilight of the Gods).

Song in "Gig at Froyle Mill," The last four lines of this poem is the chorus of the song Tony chose at random, to sing to some Hampshire cows. One of the many, fine but very sad songs, to emerge from the American Civil War.

South Downs: Is a range of chalk hills that extends for about 260 square miles across the south-eastern coastal counties of England from the Itchen Valley of Hampshire in the west to Beachy Head, near Eastbourne, East Sussex, in the east.

Spelsbury Church: Tony came upon—by chance—this lost ancient church, while actually lost himself in The Cotswolds! This Anglican of All Saints' Church was originally Norman with a central tower, built around 1100. In about 1200 transepts were added, but during the 13th century the Early English Gothic nave was built on the site of the Norman chancel. The nave is flanked by north and south aisles. The present west doorway in the tower and several of the windows in the aisles are early 14th century. In 1706 the 1st Earl of Lichfield had the bell tower restored. In 1740 the 2nd Earl of Lichfield had the chancel rebuilt. In 1774 the 4th Earl of Lichfield had the nave and aisles remodelled. The chancel was rebuilt again in 1851.

St. Botolph-without-Bishopsgate: A Church of England church on the west side of Bishopsgate in the City of London, first mentioned in 1212. It survived the Great Fire of London in 1666, and was rebuilt in 1724-9. The church is on the west side of Bishopsgate near Liverpool Street station. In the Middle Ages the site was just outside the city walls near the "Bishop's Gate" after which the street is named. St Botolph was a patron saint of travellers, so it was an appropriate dedication for a church near a city gate. There were three other churches of St Botolph in medieval London, at Billingsgate, Aldgate and Aldersgate.

The Admiral Benbow: Refers to the name of an Inn, referred by Tony in this poem "Anything That's Going" [page 112], which is the name of the Inn where the Louis Stevenson book, *Treasure Island* begins. Jack Hawkins is the main character, son of the owners. The real Admiral John Benbow (10 March 1653 – 4 November 1702) was an English officer in the Royal Navy. He joined the navy aged 25 years, seeing action against Algerian pirates before leaving and joining the merchant navy where he traded until the Glorious Revolution of 1688, whereupon he returned to the Royal Navy and was commissioned.

The Burren - An extraordinary and beautiful part of County Clare (West of Ireland). Often described as "Moonscape," being a vast, mountainous area of pale grey limestone.

The Erlkonig: In German, "Der Erlkönig" is a poem by Johann Wolfgang von Goethe. It depicts the death of a child assailed by a supernatural being, the Erlking or "Erlkönig" (suggesting the literal translation "alder king"). It was originally composed by Goethe as part of a 1782 Singspiel entitled *Die Fischerin*.

The Fens: Also known as the Fenland(s), are a naturally marshy region in eastern England. Most of the fens were drained several centuries ago, resulting in a flat, damp, low-lying agricultural region. They reach into two of the nine official regions of England (the East of England and the East Midlands), four counties (Lincolnshire, Cambridgeshire, Norfolk and a small area of Suffolk).

The King's Men: [see The Rollright Stones].

The Peddars Way: A long distance footpath in Norfolk, England. It is 46 miles long and follows the route of a Roman road. It has been suggested by more than one writer that it was not created by the Romans but was an ancient trackway [possible 3,000 years old], a branch or extension of the Icknield Way, used and remodelled by the Romans. The name is said to be derived from the Latin pedester – on foot. It is first mentioned on a map of 1587 AD. It starts at Knettishall Heath in Suffolk, England (near the Norfolk-Suffolk border, about 4 miles east of Thetford), and it links with the Norfolk Coast Path at Holme-next-the-Sea.

The False Knight on the Road: Reference to a tradition song, adapted by John Gower, from earlier stories. Also a reference to Steeleye Span's song of the same name. The False Knight was in fact the devil posing as a knight, woe-betide those that didn't see through his disguise.

The Five Sisters window: The Five Sisters window dominates the north transept of York Minster. The transepts and crossing now form the oldest part of the present cathedral, and were built in the Early English style. The north transept was finished probably by 1255. The window was completed by 1260, and is the oldest complete window in the Minster. It is also said to be the largest single composition in Grisaille glass anywhere in the world. It consists of five lights, each of 53 feet by 5 feet, and (originally) thirteen compartments.

The ship of fools: Is an allegory that has long been a fixture in Western literature and art. The allegory depicts a vessel populated by human inhabitants who are deranged, frivolous, or oblivious passengers aboard a ship without a pilot, and seemingly ignorant of their own direction. This concept makes up the framework of the 15th century book Ship of Fools (1494) by Sebastian Brant, which served as the inspiration for Bosch's famous painting, Ship of Fools: a ship—an entire fleet at first—sets off from Basel to the paradise of fools. In literary and artistic compositions of the 15th and 16th centuries, the cultural motif of the ship of fools also served to parody the 'ark of salvation' as the Catholic Church was styled.

The Whispering Knights: [see The Rollright Stones].

"Tom" Paxton, Thomas Richard: (born October 31, 1937) Is an American folk singer and singer-songwriter who has had a music career spanning more than fifty years. In 2009, Paxton received a Grammy Lifetime Achievement Award.

Tony Bird: A folk rock singer-songwriter who was born and grew up in Nyasaland (now Malawi) in Southern Africa. He is known for his Dylanesque vocals and for his songs which describe life in colonial Nyasaland from a progressive anti-colonial point of view. He made his first solo performances at the Space Theatre in Cape Town where his unique African style was reviewed favorably by press and promoters. He recorded two albums in the 70s. His comeback CD Sorry Africa, released in 1990 on Rounder Records in the USA and Mountain Records in Europe and Africa, included the hit song "Mango Time," which describes the happiness of the mangoes being ripe, once a year.

Troubadour Club: Situated at 263-267 Old Brompton Road in Earls Court, London, established in 1954, is one of the last remaining coffee houses of its era in London, with a club room in the cellar famous as one of the primary venues of the British folk revival in the late 1950s and 1960s. The club was one of several London coffee house venues at which notable musicians played; other such venues included Les Cousins and Bunjies. With Nigel Barker, Tony ran a show from 1968 to 1976, where I first met Tony.

"...upon Westminster Bridge:" A sonnet by William Wordsworth. Full title is "Composed upon Westminster Bridge, written September 3, 1802 describing London and the River Thames, viewed from Westminster Bridge in the early morning. It was first published in the collection *Poems, in Two Volumes* in 1807.

White Ensign: A flag flown by warships of the British Royal Navy.

Walsingham: Refers to Walsingham Abbey famous for its spectacular ruins of the mediaeval Priory and place of pilgrimage. Walsingham has a long history of religious pilgrimage, by tradition dating back to the 11th century, but possibly even more ancient, with origins in pre-Christian practice.

Warwick: The main town in the county of Warwickshire, England. The town lies upon the River Avon, 11 miles (18 km) south of Coventry and just west of Leamington Spa and Whitnash.

Yeats' Tower: Thoor Ballylee Castle, is a fortified, 15th (or 16th) century Anglo-Norman tower house built by the septs de Burgo, or Burke, near the town of Gort in County Galway, Ireland. It is also known as Yeats' Tower because it was once owned and inhabited by the poet William Butler Yeats.

INDEX OF TITLES AND FIRST LINES

Titles are in bold with first lines in italics.

A bit like	*92*
A Gig	**79**
A little girl came in from the garden:	*94*
A poem for Gesa her group of girls,	*26*
A River with G	**26**
A work of extraordinary...	*59*
Across the path that leads	*27*
Alan & Luke	**14**
All Night Story	**49**
All White Cat	**17**
An old, shaggy, black and white dog	*14*
And in our World where concrete, steel, glass and neon	*6*
Another River Song	**54**
Answering Dad Back	**126**
Answers on a Postcard	**12**
Anything That's Going!	**112**
Arcadia	**18**
Arriving at night, we went straight to a pint	*80*
As I roved out one morning,	*67*
As I went for a lone, kerb-kicking stroll Last night,	*72*
At the third rich seam I found	*66*
At what time do the House Martins rise?	*20*
Autumn	**55**
Autumn — What I always loved!	*55*
Bedside Companions	**98**
Butterflies fly in a wobbly way	*16*
Butterlies / Soldiers	**16**
Callum's Story	**15**
Came on the feast of Candlemas,	*57*
Catdream	**25**
Cave Carvings	**6**
Change of Plea	**10**
Charlie Blue	**22**

Christmas Cheer in Dryburgh Road, Putney	**70**
Cill Siolan bridge in the evening sun,	*41*
Clearing out his cupboard under the stairs,	*124*
Comedy of Manners	**52**
Concentrate!	**24**
Cross faces are the finest things,	*21*
Dalmatian	**72**
Derry woman, Mum, knocked about	*52*
DON BE 100	**100**
Double Take	**19**
Down by the graveyard, you're bound to see him	*39*
Dusty cloaks of russet, red and green,	*83*
Ely Cathedral	**57**
Ennis Summer	**38**
Et Tu Leonardo?	**94**
Faery Tale, Connemara	**33**
Fifteen Miles	**39**
For The Lady with The Unicorn and	*63*
For the Spelsbury Children	**65**
From the Track Through the Pines to the Copper Sea	**119**
From the upstairs window at Midnight,	*73*
Frost again, in fact ICE!	*71*
German Fairy-Tale Winter Tour	**84**
Gig at Froyle Mill	**66**
Girl on the pavement	*110*
Great Spotted or Green and Decker	**24**
Hackpen Hill-Avebury	**61**
Here's a bash at an animal fable,	*24*
Here's a wise owl	*28*
Holding a mic.	*44*
HOUSE INSURANCE FORM – PUTNEY AREA – LONDON	*104*
House Martins	**20**
I am a Rose Thief, unashamed.	*109*
I call him the Bernard Shaw of the park bench—	*36*

I came across, in my lined diary	*17*
I came to Connemara	*33*
I cannot go to The Rollright Stones,	*62*
I often take the Uke about	*82*
I seem to have lost my Upateight	*101*
I went into the garden late	*19*
I'll really have to charge this car,	*101*
I'm amazed how many people don't know	*111*
I've lost my list of "Things to do,"	*98*
Icon	**110**
If all the music were hoovered up,	*78*
If All the Music...	**78**
In a Saucepan	**32**
In a saucepan, we caught a crab,	*32*
In plenty of time, arrive Dover,	*84*
In the Old People's Home,	
I walked through what I call the "Salon,"	*112*
It was the Poppers that did it!	*99*
JAK 359W	**102**
Jealousy	**99**
Jumpers	**106**
Kids can hide me	*30*
Kilsheelan Bridge	**41**
Lines from the Underground	**93**
Little tin box with a slit for a coin	*65*
Loading bricks in Dryburgh Road,	*70*
London Thunder	**73**
Luxembourg* transmitted magic	**123**
Make a List, Lest Ye Be Lost	**98**
Medieval Music — Hanover Station	**83**
Mediterranean weather	*37*
Met a 95	
Midnight Feast	**30**
Monarch of the Roof-tops	**37**
Mother Nature must have made	*24*
Must Go Home	**21**

My pin-up	*98*
Names of Trees	**111**
New Life Resolution	**101**
New Neighbours	**75**
No Time	**75**
No Webs!	**27**
NOT TO MENTION THE WEATHER IN THE WEST:	*51*
Now that Russell Hoban's gone,	*2*
Occupation:	**104**
On the way home,	*93*
On this space-suspended spinning stone,	*114*
On Tour in Ulster	**50**
Only Joking	**101**
"Paint the back door blue" she said,	*22*
Paths to the Sun	**95**
Pencil	**91**
Poem For Mr. Boyd - the Poet	**124**
Poems should be spun with lights and pictures,	*88*
Poets	**89**
Poets are a nawful pest, best	*89*
Presentation	**88**
Radio	**123**
Recording the Sea	**44**
River of Kids	**13**
"ROLL of HONOUR" For Two World Wars	**74**
Run of the Mill	**76**
Run of the mill they call me.	*76*
Scribbling with this commandeered pencil	*91*
Sensuous poem	*108*
Serious Rain	**43**
Seven Years to Draw a Swan	**114**
Short Fruity Poem	**108**
So where IS this stone?? All the guide book said:	*56*
Spelsbury Church	**63**
Standing Stone - Cornwall - Fourth Century A.D.	**56**
...Street Deal	**36**

The boy who likes eggs for their own sake	*15*
The first glass, with Colin, hitchhiker,	*43*
The Five Sisters Window	**59**
The horses on Hackpen-three white, the other black	*61*
The Isle of Emerald, Ruby and...	**48**
The landscape of America	*3*
The Music	**82**
The Peddars Way	**67**
The phone rang... with:	*79*
The Poetry Festival	**80**
The river normally wending its way	*49*
The Rollright Stones	**62**
The Rose Thief	**109**
The Squatters moved in quietly,	*75*
"There was once a coach firm called CLATTERYS,"	*45*
There Was a Time Before the TV	**60**
There was a time before the TV,	*60*
There were spider kids poised in the corners	*13*
There's no membership fee	*90*
They all dream of a special prize:	*25*
Though	*18*
Though only a car...	*102*
Through the Hampshire hills and hop-fields green	*54*
Through the road-block, R.U.C. men	*50*
To Draw Or Not To Draw	**92**
To Ireland	**45**
To Yeats' Tower where fear of death	*40*
Today I saw you, late as usual,	*75*
Treasurer	**90**
Trilogy About America	**3**
Truman, Trussell,	*74*
Two swallows on the gutter	*38*
What have you achieved this week?	*126*
What they call "Rag Rugs" are cheap.	*106*
When I was a lad, must have been about ten,	*119*
Whirligig	**71**
Who was the first to look at the sky	*12*
Without Surprise	**28**
"WONDER & BE GLAD"	*100*

Wrote a Carol for the Radio 42
Wrote a carol for the Radio— 42

Yeats' Tower 40
Your 'onour I admit, I am to blame! 10

4-Jul-13 2

ABOUT THE AUTHOR

Tony Maude, the London, UK, based poet and musician has been writing for and working with children and adults for over 40 years. Educated at New College, Oxford in Modern Languages, he works throughout Europe in schools, libraries, universities, arts festivals and theatres. Tony has released 5 albums as a songwriter. *Between the River and the Stars* is his first book of poems. He divides his time between Putney, London and Co. Clare, in the west of Ireland.

www.tonymaude.com

www.ingramcontent.com/pod-product-compliance
Lightning Source LLC
Chambersburg PA
CBHW080508110426
42742CB00017B/3040